# Choose the Best House for You

## The Feng Shui Checklist™

**The Feng Shui Checklist Work Sheets
Can Be Found on Pages 19–24**

# Choose the Best House for You
## House for You
### The Feng Shui Checklist™

Over 150 illustrated problems and solutions in an easy
to use checklist for evaluating a house you are
planning to buy, rent, or are currently living in

First Edition
**ISBN # 0-9743008-1-0**

**Library of Congress Control Number: 2003096242**

*Published by:*

Elliot Jay Tanzer
P. O. Box 891924, Temecula, CA 92589-1924

☯

To order additional copies of
*Choose the Best House for You: The Feng Shui Checklist*™ call:
(310) 281-6798, or order on-line: www.ElliotTanzer.com

## ~ Acknowledgments ~

I have been fortunate to receive the teachings of feng shui from grandmasters, masters and those who some day will be masters and grandmasters. To all of these individuals I am greatly indebted. But first and foremost I am indebted to my friend James Allyn Moser, former CEO of the Feng Shui Warehouse. His encouragement to begin my training and the thoroughness of the Five-Day Practitioner's Training he, and fellow practitioner, Seann Xenja presented provided me with a solid foundation.

James, as a promoter and the convenor of four International Feng Shui Conferences, has also given me the opportunity to further my studies of Black Sect Tantric Buddhist Feng Shui with Grandmaster Prof. Lin Yun and to tap the wealth of information regarding the use of the Luo P'an and the application of Eight Mansion and Flying Star Feng Shui formulas with Grandmaster Yap Cheng Hai, Master Peter Leung, Master Raymond Lo, and many others including Prof. Jes T. Lim, David Twicken and Lillian Too.

I also have great appreciation for the remarkable lineage of teachers who have preserved and perpetuated feng shui teachings from their origins through many centuries of refinement. With this in mind I wish to acknowledge my deep gratitude to all my teachers who have assisted me throughout my life which include my first teachers, my parents, David and Pauline, and my brother Michael.

I also want to acknowledge my son Rama for his refinements to the cover art, as creative designer for the Feng Shui Master Formula™ Study Cards, and his skill as webmaster in designing my website ElliotTanzer.com. And a special thanks for editorial support from Joan Wilcox and Karen Stover.

And of course I am thankful for the loving support of my youngest son, Andrew, and lovely lady Holly.

My life has been truly blessed a thousand fold.

*Elliot Tanzer*

Temecula, CA
October 2003

# Contents

# *Your First Steps to Good Feng Shui*

## Everything is Integral to Everything Else

Health, Wealth &
Great Good Fortune

# Guidelines to Energy Flow Analysis

## What is Ch'i and How It Flows

*Feng he, ri li, shui qing, shu mao.*
Mild wind, warm sun, clear water, lush vegetation,
the essential ingredients for a site with good Feng Shui.
~~ H.H. Prof. Thomas Lin Yun

In this book, you will learn how to use feng shui principles and methods to evaluate the energy of your property, your neighborhood, how your home is designed, and how the rooms are configured. You will learn to identify how the energy flows to, through and around your home and what areas of your home have beneficial feng shui and in which areas the feng shui is detrimental with suggestions how to transform derimental energy flow to become beneficial.

### Searching For a Home With Good Feng Shui

The Feng Shui Checklist actually began when a student said, "I'm house hunting. Do you have any feng shui guidelines?" I said, "sure," and typed up a one page list. The one page list soon grew to the 166 questions that comprise the Feng Shui Checklist making this the most comprehensive list of energy flow problems compiled anywhere. An invaluable resource of feng shui remedies focused on the physical reality of a house: the energy of the property, the energy of the home in relationship to its surroundings, and the energy of how the home was constructed.

The Feng Shui Checklist on the following pages also grew out of my own search for a good feng shui home. In our search we looked at many homes and noted their many problems. These problems and solutions kept getting added to the original list of feng shui guidelines. These problems and solutions were constantly being organized and re-organized according to different categories as listed in the Table of Contents.

### What Is Ch'i?

Ch'i is the Chinese word for energy. Everything animate and inanimate, real or conceptual, has ch'i. Different people have different ch'i. Different animals have their different ch'i. A nation has its ch'i and a religion has its ch'i. There is roadway ch'i, rock ch'i, locational ch'i, and vocational ch'i. There is soft-yin ch'i and hard-yang ch'i. There's children ch'i. Male and female ch'i. Different foods have different ch'i. Differing circumstances have differing ch'i. To identify the ch'i of anything animate or inanimate, real or conceptual, is to understand its essential nature. Ch'i is the Isness of whatever is – its essence. There is perhaps no other study more important than the study of ch'i if your concern is good health and success in all areas of your life.

## Why Feng Shui

The study of how the ch'i in our working and living environments effect us is called feng shui (füng sch'way). The art and science of feng shui is based on many thousands of years of observation and application. Knowing the feng shui of how our environment effect us is also the study of how we can alter the ch'i flow of our environment to be more beneficial. Feng shui techniques allow us to mitigate the negative influences while enhancing the positive ones.

The Chinese words "feng" and "shui" are actually descriptions of ch'i flow. "Feng" means wind and "shui" means water. Feng-wind, refers to the invisible or intangible ch'i that flows through a space. Shui-water, is the visible, more tangible flow of ch'i. The study of feng shui encompasses all the ways that ch'i in the home environment can have an effect on the inhabitants of that environment.

## How Do You Know If You Have Good Feng Shui?

The answer is: Are you happy and healthy? Are you enjoying great prosperity, or at least more than enough to provide for your needs? Do you have a committed, mutually supportive and satisfying personal relationship? Are your children thriving, respectful, and socially conscious? Are they creative and successful academically? If your answer is "yes" to each of these questions, then the answer to the original question is: "Yes, the house you are living in has good feng shui."

If your house does not have good feng shui for wealth, you are always running to catch up. If your house does not have good feng shui for health, you are tired and stressed more often than not. If your house does not have good feng shui for relationship harmony, you are single (which in some cases might be a life style choice), or you are in an unhappy relationship and might as well be living alone. If you have children and they are a source of ongoing stress, grief, and melodrama, your home has unfavorable feng shui .

Of course the feng shui of your house may be just good enough that you are doing well in some of these areas while not doing well in others; or, not doing well in one area may be distracting you from doing even better in all the others.

## The Nature of Life-Giving Energy, Sheng Ch'i

All beneficial ch'i is pleasant, uplifting and inspiring. It is anything that is pleasant to smell, hear or look at. Beneficial ch'i flow is smooth, graceful and its movement can be described as meandering. Meandering ch'i is easy to accumulate. Meandering ch'i brings nourishment. Anything that allows us to relax and encourages us to interact with others harmoniously reflects good ch'i and good ch'i flow. Good ch'i enables us to maintain concentration, productivity and enthusiasm, to enjoy restful sleep, intimate relationships, and moments of quiet reflection and contemplation. Good ch'i flow attracts opportunity and the aware-

The Chinese philosopher Hsu said that ch'i comes from ling, which are tiny, airborne particles or molecular charges that circulate in the universe and enter the womb at conception. When we are born, ling becomes ch'i; when we die, our ch'i returns to the limitless universal ling.
~~ Jami Lin,
*The Feng Shui Anthology: Contemporary Earth Design*

ness to take advantage of opportunity when it comes our way. An environment that has meandering ch'i flow is harmonious to live in. Everything in nature that is vibrant and joyous is an example of life-giving ch'i. Calm, meandering, pleasant ch'i is the standard against which all other ch'i can be measured. The Chinese words for life-giving ch'i is "sheng ch'i" – the source of good ch'i.

## Sha Ch'i – Noxious Energy That Takes Life Away

When ch'i moves too fast, too slow, if it is excessive or deficient, if it is overbearing or distracting, if it is any extreme, it is an example of sha ch'i. Sha ch'i is noxious, stress producing, and unhealthy. Sha ch'i undermines our vitality, focus, enthusiasm, and emotional equanimity. Sha ch'i is also referred to as "killing ch'i." It can be said with certainty that sha ch'i takes life away.

In evaluating a home we are currently living in, or in our search for a property and home design that supports a fulfilling life, we must be conscious of the environmental sources of unhealthy, sha ch'i. An important concern of feng shui diagnosis, while encouraging good ch'i to accumulate, is also to identifying the presence of sha ch'i and then consider ways to transform it to beneficial life-giving sheng ch'i.

## Hidden Arrows – A Type of Sha Ch'i

In contrast to life-giving, smooth flowing, meandering ch'i, anything in nature that moves in a straight line is a form of sha ch'i. Sha ch'i that comes from straight lines, sharp and pointy-edges or angles is called "hidden arrows." Some call hidden arrows "poison arrows." Hidden arrows or poison arrows "shoot" ch'i rapidly in the direction the "arrow" is pointing.

Chi travels in a curve. When it is forced into a straight line, it acts like a bullet from a gun or an arrow from a bow that threatens to wound anything at the receiving end. Feng Shui strives to protect a space or site from these secret arrows.

~~ Angel Thompson,
*The Feng Shui Anthology: Contemporary Earth Design,*
edited by Jami Lin

The sha ch'i called "hidden arrows" is destructive. This can be seen when we compare a gently flowing stream to a rushing river. A fast moving river strips the trees from its banks. Or when we compare an animal peacefully foraging in a forest compared to a panicked animal crashing through the same forest breaking branches and trampling foliage underfoot. A straight line enables ch'i to flow too fast. The natural human response to a "hidden arrow" whether a flash flooding river or an animal raging out of control is to get out of the way as quickly as possible. The need for security and feeling secure motivates many of the suggested feng shui solutions.

The presence of "hidden arrows" in the home elicits the same response of getting out of danger's way. For example: if you were seated in your dining room eating dinner and someone was standing in the corner pointing a bow and arrow at you, understandably you would be tense and nervous. Even if it was a statue of the beautiful huntress Diana with her bow and arrow carved out of stone, you would still feel uneasy. Without too much hesitation you would soon get up and point the arrow in a different direction – a direction away from you.

Some "hidden arrows" are quite obvious while others are very abstract. They are embedded in the environment and are not clearly perceived as an actual arrow shaft with an actual life-threatening, sharp-pointed arrowhead. Consequently, many "hidden arrows" are often ignored by the conscious or rational mind.

Though ignored by the conscious-rational mind, the subconscious-emotional mind continues to squirm in its little understood attempt to get out of the way of danger – to get out of the "line of fire." People often sense something is wrong but have difficulty identifying the problem. Whether an angle of the wall, a sharp corner of furniture, or a pointy-leaf plant, the subconscious prepares for the inevitable impact of this "arrow" which in reality will never fly forth. To the subsconscious-emotional mind there is no differentiation between the illusion of danger and the dangerous situation that is real. The subconscious will do whatever is necessary to avoid the danger without the more consciously aware rational mind necessarily being aware of what evasive action may have been set into motion.

### How "Hidden Arrows" Undermine Health

This constant tensing in anticipation of being hit and hurt keeps the adrenals 'fight and flight' response at high alert. Along with the adrenal glands secretion of adrenaline, the 'fight and flight' hormone, other symptoms of a body in tension are: accelerated heart beat, high blood pressure, rapid and shallow breathing. If this tense posturing continues for prolong periods of time, the immune system is ultimately undermined and all matter of health problems are likely to emerge.

At the same time the immune system is weakening, the area of the body in direct line of the "hidden arrow" becomes inflamed. It eventually collapses when put under real pressure during sports or even normal everyday activities. The blame is quickly put on the activity instead of on the real culprit, the environmental presence of a "hidden arrow." Like all sha ch'i, "hidden arrows" need to be removed, blocked or deflected.

### Ch'i Flows In Many Ways

The first challenge of feng shui diagnosis is to determine how ch'i flows to, through and around the home and then to identify if it is beneficial or detrimental. Beneficial ch'i flow can be enhanced, energized, or enjoyed just as it is. But of the utmost importance is to identify the problem areas that are causing unfortunate sha ch'i. Once you identified the problem areas, your next challenge is to find solutions. As stated, solutions (remedies, cures, or countermeasures) are ways to regulate the ch'i flow to ensure that it flows smoothly and abundantly.

In nature, rivers, mountains, valleys, trees, meadows, pathways, and other landscape features are all channels for ch'i flow. In cities, this translates as roadways, alleyways, buildings, and open spaces. Inside a home, ch'i flows through an "internal landscape" of doors, windows, stairways, and hallways,

"In Feng Shui, streets are seen as 'waterways', channeling Ch'i at a variety of speeds, from the raging rivers of interstate highways, to the meandering streams of country roads, to the stop-and-go quagmires of city intersections."
~~ Terah Kathryn Collins, *The Western Guide to Feng Shui: Creating Balance, Harmony, and Prosperity in Your Environment*

and is assisted or blocked by furniture, accessories, and structural components of the house. As we have seen, when ch'i flow to, through or around a home is obstructed, stagnant, or excessive, the inhabitants are adversely effected. In contrast smooth and abundant ch'i flow through the outside landscape and the internal landscape results in a sense of well-being and self-assurance. A sense of being in the flow. The goal of feng shui is to attract, capture and hold on to the good ch'i long enough to be enjoyed as a benefit before it flows on again.

## Feng Shui to the Rescue

The home can be compared to a container – a container that holds energy. If the container is full of holes, the energy "leaks out" and we run around frenetically trying to get back that which was lost. We try and try until we collapse with exhaustion or give up in despair.

Imagine carrying a bucket to a well, filling it to the brim, walking home and discovering the bucket is empty because the bucket was riddled with holes of varous sizes. Before returning to the well, you very cleverly patch the holes in the bucket. Consequently, your next trip to the well is a great success.

Your home is similar to the bucket – an "energy container" with many holes in it. By using feng shui ch'i diagnosis, instead of racing madly to keep filling the leaky container, we can instead identify the "energy leaks" and then devise a plan for "patching the holes" in the container. By removing, blocking or deflecting sha ch'i we make the container, the home, stronger. Problem solving solutions are called remedies, cures or countermeasures. Solutions to make a good situation even better are called enhancements or energizers.

If the identified sources of sha ch'i cannot be removed, blocked or deflected, a decision has to be made as to how serious the problem is as some sources of sha ch'i are more detrimental than others. Once the problem has been identified, almost all situations can be easily remedied. In the worst situations the only solution is to pack up and move. The Feng Shui Checklist format of this book was designed to enable you to evaluate all the possible ways sha ch'i can be found in and around the home.

## Creating Harmonious Ch'i Flow

Everything felt by our senses is evaluated by both the conscious-rational mind as well as with the subconscious-feeling mind. It is a natural inclination for living things to be attracted to that which is soft, curvey, accommodating and to feel rebuffed or put off by that which is hard, angular, and felt as aggressive and uninviting. By improving the household ch'i, you improve your own personal ch'i. By applying feng shui principles and methods, you will be able to create beneficial ch'i flow in the home and enjoy a happy and harmonious life.

# Some examples of ch'i flow which are the basis for the questions on the Feng Shui Checklist

### Life-Giving (Sheng) Ch'i – Ch'i Flow Which Can Be Enhanced

• **Meandering ch'i** – moves along casually and gracefully. It is ch'i that is the most nourishing and easiest to accumulate. Meandering ch'i leads to harmony which expresses itself as good health, prosperity and nurturing relationships. It encourages focus and stability and translates as a natural rhythm. Meandering ch'i signifies the ideal. It is pleasant, calming and enjoyable. The ch'i of all things can be evaluated and compared to this standard.

• **Expansive ch'i** – is open, light and gives a feeling of spaciousness and comfort.

• **Positive symbolic ch'i** – are images, items or certain patterns which are psychologically uplifting, inspiring, and motivating.

### Forms of Sha – Ch'i That Needs Adjusting

Sha ch'i is detremental. Most feng shui solutions are designed to prevent sha ch'i and increase good, sheng ch'i. Sha ch'i can express itself in any of the following ways:

• **Fast moving ch'i** – needs to be slowed down. Fast moving ch'i from long hallways and heavily trafficked roadways can over-energize the adrenals and leads to physical fatigue.

• **Excessive ch'i** – needs to be diffused. Excessive ch'i from large windows and large spaces is over-stimulating and leads to loss of focus and nervous exhaustion.

• **Obstructed ch'i** – needs to be unblocked. Obstructed ch'i from clutter, blank walls, and poorly positioned furniture causes frustration and leads to stress, anxiety, and inertia.

• **Stagnant ch'i** – needs to be freshened. Stagnant ch'i from standing water or poor ventilation is unhealthy, devitalizing, and leads to depression and poor health.

• **Compressed ch'i** – needs to be redirected. Compressed ch'i from overhead beams or slanted ceilings inflames the area of the body "under pressure," making it vulnerable to injury or illness.

• **Chopping ch'i** – needs to be deflected or diffused. Chopping ch'i from overhead fans generate fear and uncertainty. Ceiling fans directly above the head disturbs the heart and nervous system.

• **Split ch'i** – needs to be unified. Split ch'i from pillars and structural supports is disorienting and leads to confusion, misunderstanding, arguments, and indecisiveness.

• **Excessive yin ch'i** – needs to be dried out and warmed up. Excessive yin ch'i from too much water, lush foliage, or dark shadows encourages mold growth and poor air quality and leads to problems of the urinary tract, kidneys, and lymphatic system.

• **Excessive yang ch'i** – needs to be moistened and cooled down. Excessive yang ch'i from too much heat or bright lights leads to frantic activity, over heating, and dehydration which stresses the heart, raises the blood pressure, dries the kidneys, and exhausts the adrenals.

• **Negative symbolic ch'i** – are images, items or certain patterns which have negative associations (death, divorce, sickness, fears, and so on). Negative symbols need to be removed and can result in depression, anxiety, relationship disharmony and ill-health. Symbolic ch'i should be positive and uplifting.

Remedies are also called cures, and can be chi *activators, adjusters, enhancers, stimulators, lifters, stabilizers, or deflectors,* depending upon the correction needed. When placing feng shui remedies, it is especially important to remember that they are to be put in place with a sincere heart while setting a clear intention.

~~ Holly Ziegler,
*Sell Your Home FASTER with Feng Shui: Ancient Wisdom to Expedite the Sale of Real Estate*

# The Feng Shui Checklist Procedure

## How to Use This Book

We shape our dwellings, and afterwards
our dwellings shape us.
~~ Sir Winston Churchill

The Feng Shui Checklist will help you to easily and quickly make an accurate and comprehensive evaluation of any home you are considering buying, renting or are currently living in. In just a short time you will know about the positive ch'i aspects of the house and its property, and about the negative ch'i aspects. When you discover sha ch'i – ch'i that could create disharmony – you will learn how correct the problem to get positive ch'i flowing again. You might also discover that some problems have no acceptable solutions. If there are many unsolvable ch'i problems, it is advisable to move on until you find a home with a strong feng shui foundation.

### A Strong Feng Shui Foundation

With a strong feng shui foundation you're home will provide you with the maximum security and support in all your endeavors from restful regenerative sleep to intimate romantic interludes, from inspiring you to be successful in all your projects to your children achieving their academic best. In short, whatever, you imagine the best life for yourself to be, choosing a home with a strong feng shui foundation will ensure you a home that will support you during the inevitable ups and downs that come with our relatively brief stay on planet Earth.

### My Suggestion

I would suggest that you photocopy the Feng Shui Checklist Work Sheets on pages 19–24. This will help you keep an accurate record. Write the address of the house under consideration in the space provided. If you are house hunting, you may want to make a dozen photocopies in preparation of looking at many homes before deciding on the one that is best for you.

It is also suggested that you obtain accurate floor plans or at least a fairly accurate sketch so you can analyze the layout of the house, room configurations, and relationship of doors and windows in regard to their effect on areas of the house that will be frequently used.

### Perfect Feng Shui? Not Likely

Drawing from the different levels of feng shui evaluation we should consider ourselves lucky if we can find a home that has at least 70% good feng

shui. The remaining 30% of feng shui problems should be resolvable by applying the various feng shui techniques of ch'i adjustment. Outside the home ch'i adjustments can often be made by remodeling or by landscaping. Ch'i adjustments can be accomplished inside the home either by remodeling or by decorating. In my next book, *The Feng Shui Checklist: Designing the Best Home for You*, I will describe ways to use interior design to enhance beneficial ch'i and what design elements to avoid.

The vast majority of feng shui problems listed in the Feng Shui Checklist can be remedied, though there are a few extreme situations that make a home totally uninhabitable (House Problems Without Remedies, page 27). With each feng shui problem listed I do my best to provide you with the parameters to guide you in making a correct evaluation of how serious the problem may be, and how to apply the appropriate remedy. When in doubt, call an experienced feng shui practitioner. Or go to my website, ElliotTanzer.com and click on "Feng Shui Clinic" where you can E-mail me your questions.

### Using the Feng Shui Checklist to Discover Problems & Determine Solutions

Our first concern is to reveal the problems inherent in the dwelling. Our next concern is to determine if the identified problem is resolvable or to what degree of effort may be required to resolve such a problem. And if it is even worth the effort.

The questions listed in the Feng Shui Checklist are mostly examples of feng shui problems that can be found in and around the home environment. Some of the questions are phrased in the negative in order to keep all the "yes" answers consistent. As we are mostly concerned with locating problems that need to be remedied, read through the questions of the Feng Shui Checklist and make a ☑ in the first row of boxes only if there is a **PROBLEM** and leave the box blank if there is no problem. Making only a check mark for problems will also help to keep the work sheets uncluttered as you go back to review the problems and consider the solutions.

After you have answered all the questions, go back over your list and review the problems of the house by reading the page numbers provided at the end of each question. Here you will find a description of each problem in greater detail, why it is a problem, and how to evaluate the severity of the problem. After reading the description of the problem, the next paragraph will give Solutions. Here you will find suggestions on how to alter the detrimental nature of the problem and transform them into more positive, harmonious ch'i flow. As some feng shui terminology may be new to you, or to clarify the questions, it may be necessary to first read the description on the page given with a specific question in order to understand how to accurately answer the question.

After reading the Solutions given for those question you had ☑'ed in the first row of boxes, record if the problem can be easily resolved or not in the second row of boxes. If the problem CANNOT be remedied, ☑ the box to indicate the problem still remains. If the problem noted can be resolved and is no longer to be considered as a problem, leave the box unmarkeded. This way, if you decide to choose this house to live in, you can go back to the checklist to review the problem and determine which solution to apply.

Once you have answered all the questions, reviewed all the solutions. You can now ponder to what degree of severity those feng shui flaws that cannot be changed are likely to have on your life.

Searching for a home with good feng shui can at times be frustrating. Be patient and don't panic. Remember, 100% good feng shui is not probable so don't become obsessed trying to find a "perfect" feng shui home. From a feng shui point-of-view all homes have problems. Your challenge is to find the home with the best feng shui possible, identify the potential problems, consider the suggested remedies, and to remain calm in the process. Consider each candidate carefully and then choose the best home for you and your family.

*Feng – Wind*

*Shui – Water*

# THE FENG SHUI CHECKlIST PROCEDURE SUMMARIZED

---

**Before You Begin**

1. Duplicate the Feng Shui Checklist if you are evaluating more than one house.

2. If possible, obtain an accurate architect's floor plan of each house you are evaluating, or at least a fairly accurate hand-drawn sketch, showing the rooms of the house, how they relate to each other, and any unusual configurations.

**To Make Your Evaluations**

3. Answer the first eight questions of the Feng Shui Checklist – House Problems With No Solutions. If you ☑'ed any of these problems indicating the problem applies to the house in question, avoid this house and look for another.

4. The next six questions pertain to the Law of Predecesors which states that whatever happen to the previous occupants will problably happen to all future occupants. If you can determine what happened to the previous owners or tenants you may have clues as to what feng shui problems the home has and what you will need to do to remedy the situation before it becomes your problem as well.

5. The remaining 154 questions will determine if your home has at least 70% good feng shui. Only ☑ boxes in the first row if a problem applies. Leave the box empty if there is no problem. The first question are subjective in nature. The First Criteria are: Does the house conform with your basic priorities of price, size, location and your family's life-style choices. And does it feel good. Your home is a reflection of you. If you are not content with your home, your unhappiness and discomfort will undermine your personal ch'i.

6. Now you are ready to walk around the outside of the house and answer the questions regarding the influence the external landscape has on a home.

7. Then walk through the house and answer the questions regarding the influence of the internal structure and room configurations. Pay special attention to your evaluation of the entrance and the bedroom.

8. Finally consider the questions in Section III: Additional Feng Shui Secrets.

**Determining A Home's Feng Shui**

9. When you have read all the solutions to the ☑'ed boxes on the Feng Shui Checklist Worksheets you will have a clear idea of what problems the house might have. You are now ready to read the page numbers provided with each question you ☑'ed to determine if the discovered problem is easy or difficult to resolve.

10. In the second row of boxes ☑ any box if the problem cannot be solved. If the problem can be resolved, leave the box empty.

11. Before making a final decision, re-read the ☑'ed boxes in the first column, review the problems and their possible consequences, and determine if the home is the best choice for you and your family.

# Choose the Best House for You
## The Feng Shui Checklist™
Work sheets for evaluating a house you are planning
to buy, rent, or are currently living in
by Elliot Jay Tanzer

**HOUSE ADDRESS:** _____

*(Photocopy this Checklist to separately evaluate each home or apartment you are considering to rent or buy.)*

## House Problems With No Solutions

Read the following eight questions. If you answer ☑ **PROBLEM** to any of these questions – DO NOT go further. The house under consideration will bring misfortune. If you answered **NO PROBLEM** to these first eight questions, continue answering the questions that follow. If you need help answering any questions, read the page numbers first.

Before After

*NO CURES*

❑    1. Extremely odd-shaped houses lacking a clear center: crescent-shaped, extreme modular, etc.  *Page 27*

❑    2. Property on reclaimed wetlands or former garbage dumping site.  *Page 28*

❑    3. Property on a cemetery or ancient burial grounds.  *Page 28*

❑    4. Houses built on the edge of a cliff, ravine or gulch.  *Page 29*

❑    5. Houses built at the bottom of a canyon wall or under a rock overhang – "tiger's jaws."  *Page 29*

❑    6. Fast moving river, rainwater drainage ditch or roadway directly behind the house.  *Page 30*

❑    7. Houses with excessive outside noises or obnoxious smells.  *Page 30*

❑    8. Houses close to a utility pole transformer, power generator station or substation, high tension wires, microwave dish, airport radar, or a nuclear power plant.  *Page 30*

## Gathering Clues About a Home's Feng Shui

If you are dealing with a real estate agent or landlord, the answers to the following four questions should be easy to obtain. If you have the opportunity to meet the previous owners or tenants, do not be shy about asking about their life. Mark an ☑ in the box if any of these problems exist. In order to change its feng shui, you will need to find the cause of each problem that is found. You will be able to determine if the problem(s) can be remedied after you answer the remaining questions in the Feng Shui Checklist and determine what caused these problems to come to pass. If a problem cannot be remedied, ☑ the box in the second row of boxes. Even if you can remedy the problem, it is still adviseable to clear the previous owner's or tenant's energy by doing a Space Clearing as described on page 33.

Before After

❑ ❑ 9. Were the previous owners financially successful? After this house did they move up in life to a better situation (leave blank)? or did they have financial problems and move down ☑?  *Page 33*

❑ ❑ 10. Did the previous owners or tenants have relationship problems?  *Page 33*

❑ ❑ 11. Did the previous owners or tenants have serious health problems?  *Page 33*

❑ ❑ 12. Did the previous owners or tenants have other major problems to consider?  *Page 33*

## The First Criteria: Does It Meet Your Needs

The answers to the next six questions are subjective and need to be considered. Finances or other factors may dictate that the home under consideration cannot meet these personal needs. If you cannot satisfy your personal needs, it is important to satisfy as many of the other requirements of good feng shui in order to increase your prosperity or change whatever circumstance is keeping you from choosing a home you are emotionally comfortable in so you can improve your situation as soon as possible. There are no cures for these situations other than to make do and move into a home more to your liking as soon as you are able.

Before After

*NO CURES*

❏    13. Does it feel good – do you like the appearance, neighborhood, views, or whatever makes a place feel like home to you? *Page 37*

❏    14. Does it offer enough space for you (& your family's) current needs? *Page 37*

❏    15. Will it satisfy your changing needs (and the needs of your family as your family grows)? *Page 37*

❏    16. Is it in proximity to work? *Page 37*

❏    17. Does it feel safe and will it provide the opportunity for peaceful, rejuvenating sleep? *Page 37*

❏    18. If there are children, is it easy for them to get to school and after school activities without adding stressful demands on the parents? *Page 37*

## The Ideal House Site: Evaluating the Property

All the following questions should be self explanatory. They are all problems that need to be solved. Some are worded in the negative to be consistent in receiving a ☑ if the answer is "Yes, there is a Problem," or leave blank if there is no problem. After answering all the questions, read the page number after each question you marked with a ☑ to determine why it is a problem, how serious the problem is, and what the solution(s) might be. If the problem CANNOT be easily remedied, ☑ the box in the second row of boxes. If the problem can be remedied, leave the box in the second row of boxes unchecked to indicate it is no longer a problem but that you will want to review the solutions later if you choose to rent or buy this home. Now reread the ☑'s to be sure the remaining problems are not severe. Note: It may be necessary to read some problem descriptions before attempting to answer some questions (ex.: #19 and #20, and any other questions whose descriptions are not clear to you).

Before After

❏ ❏   19. Is the house NOT surrounded by the "four celestial animals" to form an "armchair" configuration? *Page 39*

❏ ❏   20. Are the "green dragon" & the "white tiger" NOT in proper balance? *Page 41*

❏ ❏   21. Is there poor soil quality and lack of greenery? *Page 43*

❏ ❏   22. Does the property look like a triangle, rhomboid or other irregular shape (not a square or rectangle? *Page 44*

❏ ❏   23. Is the house situated on the front or back third of the property? *Page 46*

❏ ❏   24. Is the house built on a mountain top – on a "dragon's head?" *Page 46*

❏ ❏   25. Is the house built too close to the ocean surf or body of water? *Page 47*

❏ ❏   26. Are there mountains or very large buildings close behind or to either side? *Page 47*

❏ ❏   27. Is the house on the end of a dead-end street or a cul-de-sac? *Page 47*

❏ ❏   28. Is the house on the outer edge of a river, roadway, freeway overpass or large circular driveways? *Page 48*

❏ ❏   29. From the front door can you see the road coming toward the home and then going away? *Page 49*

❏ ❏   30. Is the house attacked by "tiger eyes" (headlights) at night? *Page 50*

❏ ❏   31. Are cars parked pointing directly at the entrance, bedroom or other frequently used rooms? *Page 50*

❏ ❏   32. Is the house on a T-section, Y-section, or busy corner lot? *Page 50*

Before After

☐ ☐ 33. Is the house on the road without a curb or step up to the front door? *Page 51*

☐ ☐ 34. Is the house or apartment down steps below street level? *Page 51*

☐ ☐ 35. Is the house below a roadway? *Page 52*

☐ ☐ 36. Is the house at the bottom of a steep driveway or hill – an "uphill struggle?" *Page 52*

☐ ☐ 37. Is the house at the top of a steep road or driveway – "opportunities roll away?" *Page 53*

☐ ☐ 38. Is the house on a one way street? *Page 53*

☐ ☐ 39. Are there high walls or foliage so the roof of the house is hidden from the street? *Page 54*

☐ ☐ 40. Do frequently used rooms face predominantly west? *Page 54*

☐ ☐ 41. Do frequently used rooms face predominantly north? *Page 55*

☐ ☐ 42. Is there a pond in the back yard or to the right of the front door? *Page 55*

☐ ☐ 43. Is there a swimming pool? What is its shape? How is it positioned? *Page 56*

## Neighbors: Harmony in the Community

☐ ☐ 44. Do the neighboring houses "attack" each other with sharp edges, gables or rooftop edges? *Page 58*

☐ ☐ 45. Is there a "tiger's mouth" opposite your front door – "big door eats little door?" *Page 59*

☐ ☐ 46. Is your neighbor's driveway & garage door opposite your front door? *Page 59*

☐ ☐ 47. Is there a house on the same property uphill from the house you are considering? *Page 59*

☐ ☐ 48. Are there neighboring houses higher up a hill? *Page 60*

☐ ☐ 49. Are there disagreeable or disturbing neighbors? *Page 60*

☐ ☐ 50. Is the house in view of a cemetery, house of worship, hospital, mortuary or slaughter house? *Page 60*

☐ ☐ 51. Can you see church crosses, factory smoke stacks, a quarry, waste water reclamation, etc? *Page 61*

## House Structure: How Energy Flows Through the Home

☐ ☐ 52. Is the house odd-shaped: U or L-shaped (cleaver, boot), modular, etc.? *Page 65*

☐ ☐ 53. Is there a fireplace, stairway, skylight or bathroom in the center of the house? *Page 66*

☐ ☐ 54. Are there very high ceilings, cathedral or vaulted ceilings? *Page 67*

☐ ☐ 55. Are there exposed beams or roof supports? *Page 68*

☐ ☐ 56. Are there sudden changes in the height of the ceiling in the same room or from room-to-room? *Page 69*

☐ ☐ 57. Are there sloped-ceilings over sitting areas? *Page 69*

☐ ☐ 58. Are there very low ceilings? *Page 70*

☐ ☐ 59. Are there pillars or free-standing structural supports? *Page 70*

☐ ☐ 60. Is there a sunken living room or other rooms on different levels? *Page 70*

☐ ☐ 61. Are there rooms that are irregularly shaped (not square or rectangular)? *Page 71*

☐ ☐ 62. Is there a long narrow hallway? *Page 72*

☐ ☐ 63. Is there a room situated at the end of a long narrow hallway? *Page 73*

☐ ☐ 64. Is the house without a back door or windows, or are there rooms with no windows at all? *Page 73*

☐ ☐ 65. Are there rooms with excessively large windows or windows that go down to the floor? *Page 74*

☐ ☐ 66. Is there a close view of a tree trunk, lamp post or utility pole through a window? *Page 75*

☐ ☐ 67. Does the house have all doors and no windows? *Page 75*

☐ ☐ 68. Does the house have a skylight or skylights? *Page 75*

☐ ☐ 69. Are there three doorways in a row – "a pierced heart?" *Page 76*

☐ ☐ 70. Are there three interior doorways very close together? *Page 77*

❏ ❏ 71. Are there three or more doors close together leading into different directions? *Page 77*

❏ ❏ 72. Does the room have double doors? *Page 77*

❏ ❏ 73. Are there two doorways that are misaligned – "bad bite?" *Page 78*

❏ ❏ 74. Are there doorways hung at an angle – "the evil door?" *Page 78*

❏ ❏ 75. Are there "contrary doors" that open to the smallest part of a room? *Page 79*

❏ ❏ 76. Are there less important doorways that are larger than important room doorways? *Page 79*

❏ ❏ 77. Is there an "empty doorway?" *Page 80*

❏ ❏ 78. Are there "arguing" door knobs (doors that clash)? *Page 80*

❏ ❏ 79. Are there "dutch doors?" *Page 80*

❏ ❏ 80. Does any door open outward instead of inward? *Page 81*

❏ ❏ 81. Is there a spiral staircase or staircases that are steep or unsteady? *Page 81*

❏ ❏ 82. Are the streets to the house, hallways in an apartment complex, or the floor plan of the house like a maze? *Page 82*

## Attracting Opportunities: Evaluating the Entrance

❏ ❏ 83. Is the view from the front door obstructed by a wall, high mountain or high building? *Page 84*

❏ ❏ 84. Is the pathway to the front door obstructed? *Page 84*

❏ ❏ 85. Does the house lack a clearly defined pathway to the front door? *Page 85*

❏ ❏ 86. Is the pathway to the front door narrow at one end and wide at the other? *Page 86*

❏ ❏ 87. Is the pathway to the front door a long, straight line? *Page 86*

❏ ❏ 88. Is the front porch dilapidated? *Page 86*

❏ ❏ 89. Are there pillars across the front porch that give the appearance of a prison? *Page 87*

❏ ❏ 90. Is there a tree, lamp post, telephone or utility pole directly opposite the front door of the house? *Page 87*

❏ ❏ 91. Is the front entrance recessed or hidden from view? *Page 88*

❏ ❏ 92. Is there an overhanging second floor balcony or excessively large lintel over the front door? *Page 89*

❏ ❏ 93. Does the front door have glass panels or does it look strange in anyway, e.g. like a coffin lid? *Page 89*

❏ ❏ 94. Is the front door too large or too small in proportion to the front façade of the house? *Page 89*

❏ ❏ 95. Is the garage door more prominent than the front door? *Page 90*

❏ ❏ 96. Does the home lack a ming t'ang (open space) outside the front entrance of the home? *Page 90*

❏ ❏ 97. Does the home lack a ming t'ang (open space) inside the front entrance of the home? *Page 91*

❏ ❏ 98. Is their a narrow hallway leading from the front door into the house? *Page 91*

❏ ❏ 99. Is there a small foyer with a wall opposite the front door? *Page 91*

❏ ❏ 100. Is there a split-view of the inside of the house from the front door (half wall, half open room)? *Page 92*

❏ ❏ 101. Is their a beam inside across the hall or foyer near the front door? *Page 93*

❏ ❏ 102. Is there a back door or window opposite the front door? *Page 93*

❏ ❏ 103. Is there a stairway from the upper floor leading directly down to the front door? *Page 94*

❏ ❏ 104. Are there two stairways opposite the entrance way - one leading up and one down. *Page 95*

❏ ❏ 105. At street level is there a stairway leading down into the main living area of the home? *Page 95*

❏ ❏ 106. Is their a bathroom above the front entrance way? *Page 96*

❏ ❏ 107. Is the bathroom door next to or opposite the front entrance way? *Page 96*

❏ ❏ 108. Is the kitchen next to the front door? *Page 97*

❏ ❏ 109. Can you see the stove from the front door? *Page 97*

❏ ❏ 110. In an apartment building is the apartment entrance next to or opposite an elevator? *Page 98*

## Rest, Rejuvenation and Romance: Evaluating the Bedroom

Before After

☐ ☐ 111. Is it difficult for the bed to be in the Command Position? *Page 100*

☐ ☐ 112. Is there a doorway directly in front of the bed – the Coffin Position? *Page 100*

☐ ☐ 113. Are there doorways on either side of the bed? *Page 101*

☐ ☐ 114. Is there a toilet – front or back – in direct line with the bed or any part of the bed? *Page 104*

☐ ☐ 115. Is the headboard on the other side of a bathroom sharing a wall with the toilet or other plumbing? *Page 104*

☐ ☐ 116. Is the electric box, electric devices or stove on the other side of the wall from a bed's headboard? *Page 105*

☐ ☐ 117. Is the bedroom an irregular shape? *Page 106*

☐ ☐ 118. Is there a beam over the bed? *Page 106*

☐ ☐ 119. Is there a sloped-ceiling over the bed? *Page 107*

☐ ☐ 120. Is there a window behind the bed? *Page 108*

☐ ☐ 121. Is there a view from the bed into the bathroom? *Page 108*

☐ ☐ 122. Is the master bedroom in the front half of the house or extended out in front of the house? *Page 109*

☐ ☐ 123. Are there bedrooms over a garage? *Page 109*

☐ ☐ 124. Is there inadequate space to walk on either side of the bed? *Page 110*

☐ ☐ 125. Does the bed position lack equality on both sides: views, lighting, space on both sides, etc? *Page 110*

## Creating Harmony in Other Rooms of the House

☐ ☐ 126. Is the kitchen narrow and dark? *Page 113*

☐ ☐ 127. Can the cook be in the Command Position in order to see anyone coming in to the kitchen? *Page 113*

☐ ☐ 128. Is the stove opposite or adjacent to the sink, refrigerator or dishwasher? *Page 114*

☐ ☐ 129. Is there a window behind the stove or is the stove next to the back or side door? *Page 114*

☐ ☐ 130. Is there a bathroom directly above the stove? *Page 115*

☐ ☐ 131. Is the dining room table positioned between two doors? *Page 115*

☐ ☐ 132. Is the child's bed NOT in the Command Position? *Page 116*

☐ ☐ 133. Is the child's room too small to position the bed against a solid wall with space on three sides? *Page 116*

☐ ☐ 134. Is the child's desk NOT in the Command Position? *Page 116*

☐ ☐ 135. Are there large windows in the children's room? *Page 117*

☐ ☐ 136. Is there a beam over the child's bed or desk? *Page 117*

☐ ☐ 137. Is there a sloped-ceiling over the child's bed or desk? *Page 118*

☐ ☐ 138. Is the child's room upstairs and the parent's room down stairs, or is the child's room toward the back of the house and the parent's room toward the front? *Page 118*

☐ ☐ 139. Does each child NOT have a space of their own? *Page 118*

☐ ☐ 140. Is the home office NOT large enough? *Page 119*

☐ ☐ 141. Is there NOT quiet or an uplifting view from the home office window? *Page 120*

☐ ☐ 142. Is the office desk NOT in the Command Position? *Page 120*

☐ ☐ 143. Is there a window behind the desk? *Page 121*

☐ ☐ 144. Is there a toilet – front or back – in direct line of the desk or chair? *Page 121*

☐ ☐ 145. Is there a bathroom door opposite the office door? *Page 122*

☐ ☐ 146. Is the garage NOT large enough for cars, storage or other uses? *Page 122*

23

## Wealth and Partnership Areas of the Home: The Ba-gua Template

Read page 125 to learn what the Ba-gua is and how it can indicate a home's weaknesses, and how those weaknesses can be strengthened.

Before After

- ❏ ❏ 147. Is there a hill sloping down behind the house? *Page 126*
- ❏ ❏ 148. Are there missing corners of the Bagua especially the Wealth or Relationship corners? *Page 127*
- ❏ ❏ 149. Is there an overly large extension in any of the areas of the house? *Page 128*
- ❏ ❏ 150. Is the bathroom in the Wealth, Health or Partnership Areas of the house? *Page 128*
- ❏ ❏ 151. Are there back doors or large windows in the Wealth or Partnership Areas? *Page 129*
- ❏ ❏ 152. Is there a children's or in-law's room in the Partnership Area of the house? *Page 130*

### Things to Change If You Can

- ❏ ❏ 153. Are there ceiling fans over beds and sitting areas (dining table, desk, etc.)? *Page 131*
- ❏ ❏ 154. Are there louvered windows and vertical or mini-blinds? *Page 132*
- ❏ ❏ 155. Is there an electric stove or microwave oven? *Page 132*
- ❏ ❏ 156. Does the house have florescent light fixtures? *Page 132*
- ❏ ❏ 157. Are there interior or exterior stairs without risers – "floating stairs?" *Page 133*
- ❏ ❏ 158. Are there thorny or pointy-leaf plants near entrance or pathways to the house? *Page 133*

### Things to Fix Immediately

- ❏ ❏ 159. Is the plumbing without leaks? *Page 136*
- ❏ ❏ 160. Are the stove without broken burners? *Page 136*
- ❏ ❏ 161. Are the hinges, floor boards or stairs squeaky? *Page 136*
- ❏ ❏ 162. Are the windows broken or cracked? *Page 136*
- ❏ ❏ 163. Are the windows stuck? *Page 136*
- ❏ ❏ 164. Are the stairs or pathways broken? *Page 136*
- ❏ ❏ 165. Is the tap water drinkable? *Page 137*

## Change Your Location, Change Your Life
## Global Feng Shui: Your Astro*Carto*Graphy Map®

Read page 139 to learn about Astro*Carto*Graphy Maps and if your geographical location is effecting you or your family. At the time of your birth each planet left its unique imprint on different locations around the world. As each planet resonates with a different energetic pattern, your personality expression, emotional issues, career success, and health problemss will be shaped by the planet that is closest to where you live. Even the best feng shui will be undermined by difficult "planetary" influences while a home with what might be considered poor feng shui will be benefited by favorable "planetary" influences. Astro*Carto*Graphy is truly "global feng shui."

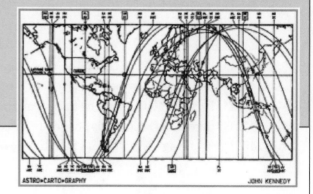

- ❏ ❏ 166. Is it difficult for you or any members your family to live in this geographical location? *Page 139*

*Section I*

# Influences of the External Environment

## The Importance of Good Feng Shui

Inside the gate there is a footpath, and the footpath must be winding. At the turning of the footpath there is an outdoor screen, and the screen must be small. Behind the screen there is a terrace, and the terrace must be level. On the banks of the terrace there are flowers, and the flowers must be fresh. Beyond the flowers is a wall, and the wall must be low. By the side of the wall, there is a pine tree and the pine tree must be old. At the foot of the pine tree there are rocks, and the rocks must be quaint.

Over the rocks there is a pavilion, and the pavilion must be simple. Behind the pavilion are bamboos, and the bamboos, must be thin and sparse. At the end of the bamboos there is a house, and the house must be secluded. By the side of the house there is a road, and the road must branch off. At the point where several roads come together, there is a bridge, and the bridge must be tantalizing to cross.

At the end of the bridge there are trees, and the trees must be tall. In the shade of the trees there is grass, and the grass must be green. Above the grass plot there is a ditch, and the ditch must be slender. At the top of the ditch there is a spring, and the spring must gurgle. Above the spring there is a hill, and the hill must be deep,

Below the hill there is a hall, and the hall must be square. At the corner of the hall there is a vegetable garden, and the vegetable garden must be big. In the vegetable garden there is a stork, and the stork must dance. The stork announces that there is a guest, and the guest must not be vulgar. When the guest arrives there is wine, and the wine must not be declined. During the service of the wine, there is merriment, and the merry guest must not want to go home.

~~ Lin Yutang, 1937
quoted by James Allyn Moser
in the Integrative School of Feng Shui Class Manual

**Abundance &
Great Good Fortune**

# House Problems With No Solutions

## Houses to Avoid

The goal of life is living in agreement with nature.
--Zeno, 4th B.C. Greek mathematician

Below I have listed some of the most detrimental and most difficult feng shui problems to solve. These are problems that any good feng shui practitioner should check before spending a lot of time on the rest of the house. Some of these problems are modern concerns which you will not find in books about traditional approaches to feng shui. These are problems that physically cannot be changed or easily remedied. Avoid renting or buying houses with problems like these.

If you are living in a home that falls in any of these categories, before you panic and move, evaluate if indeed you are having any of the difficulties described. Also consider how long you have been living in your home. If you been living there for several months to a few years and you are not having problems, 'don't fix what isn't broken.' But if you are having difficulties (though there are probably other feng shui problems), these are the one's for which there are no acceptable remedies. Again I say, consider relocating as soon as possible. The urgency of this suggestion is in proportion to the severity of health, relationship and money problems you may already be having

### Do NOT Consider Homes With These Problems
### 1. Avoid extremely odd-shaped houses or houses without a clear center.

The emphasis here is on the word "extreme." There are many U, L or S-shaped houses that have acceptable remedies using landscaping and lighting. These will be described further on (page 65, #52). The overall problem with odd-shaped houses is that they have no easily defined "center" or "heart" and are therefore fragmented and dysfunctional – they are "confused" homes. Remember, whether you are renting or owning, a home reflects the consciousness of those living within, while those living within take on the consciousness of the house.

Extremely odd-shaped houses, even U, L or S-shaped houses, are a disturbance to the subconscious as they lack a feeling and sense of wholeness. Whole shapes are squares, rectangles and even circles. Ch'i flows smoothly through whole shapes and gets confused in incomplete shapes getting stuck in corners or "getting lost" searching for the center.

The worst odd-shaped house I've visited was crescent-shaped – it looked like a "croissant." There was no way to bring it into balance. The physical

27

reality of walking from one end of the house to the other has to result in imbalance as household members career down the hallways ultimately losing equilibrium. Bizarre accidents are likely. The individual who lived in the croissant-house dived into a frozen swimming pool and broke her neck. Luckily she wasn't permanently paralyzed.

**Solution:** There are no suitable solutions for <u>extremely</u> odd-shaped houses other than remodeling them into more symmetrical configurations.

### 2. Property on reclaimed wetlands or former garbage dumping site.

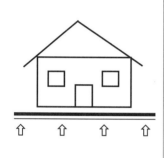

Solid ground equals stability. Beside the lack of stability, living in an area with decaying matter will eventually cause disease and ill-health as noxious gases like radon, formaldehyde, heavy metal toxins, etc. continually rise to the surface.

Consider also that as the house settles, there is a great likelihood that the foundation will crack. Little cracks are often noticeable near the corners of windows and door jams of new houses built on solid ground. How much more cracking is probable on land fill.

**Solution:** There are NOT any solutions for stabilizing land that is not solid or for neutralizing noxious gases rising from the substrata. If you can excavate down to hard rock and properly dispose of the toxic matter, then this situation can be considered.

### 3. Property on a cemetery or ancient burial grounds.

To disturb the spirit-energy of a cemetery or ancient burial grounds is to be forever disturb by the Spirits in return. Places where the dead are, or have been, buried are excessively yin (soft, dark, damp, weakening) in contrast to the best locations for homes to be built which should be yang (light, vibrant, strengthening).

Locations that were the scenes of violence such as massacres, executions, or homicides should be avoided as unsettled Spirits are attracted to such places. This will be especially amplified if the inhabitants of a dwelling had a personal connection to horrific situations occurring at that location as the "voices" of those who died will seem even louder.

Even without knowledge of what lies beneath the surface or how the location was once used, severe psychological problems (depression, suicidal, bipolar personality disorders) eventually can be expected among people living over a cemetery or ancient burial grounds.

**Solution:** At best a ritual cleansing should be conducted by an individual of high spiritual cultivation. In addition to a house clearing and house blessing to remove any remaining negativity, a ceremony should be per-

formed to assist any unsettled out-of-the-body entities to complete their journey to the other side. Best of all, avoid living in houses built in these kind of locations.

### 4. Houses built on the edge of a cliff, ravine or gulch.

Houses built on the edge of a cliff or gulch make the inhabitants feel "edgy" and come to represent a life that is being lived "on the edge." This results in nervous conditions, erratic emotions and always being anxious about finances, health and relationships. Without a "back" to the house for support the inhabitants will lack support and feel like they are always struggling to maintain stability in finances, health and relationships. The subconscious anxiously awaits the inevitable land erosion that tumbles their house off the cliff and into the ravine or gulch. The closer to the edge the more unstable the psyche.

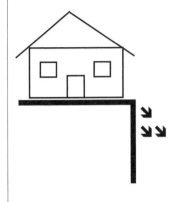

**Solutions:** Fences, hedges, and potted plants may provide some sense of containment for some people while appropriate colors and images representing those areas of the Ba-gua affected might help overcome problems in finances and relationships (page 126, #147 – Hill sloping down behind the house weakens the Ba-gua Template), but it is best to avoid homes that feel unstable for any reason.

### 5. Houses at the bottom of a canyon wall or under a rock overhang – "tiger's jaw."

Dwellings built to close to a canyon wall or even worst under a rock overhang ("tiger's jaw") live in constant anxiety of being crushed by falling rocks, literally being "devoured" by the mountain. Houses at the base of a mountainous wall in most cases do not get a full day of sun light or sun warmth which further undermines health and can contribute to a general mood of depression, despair and defeat. Strong winds are also likely to be funneled along the base of canyon walls which can add to the overall disturbance of the psyche of those living too close to a canyon wall. Backache and other back problems are also likely from trying to unconsciously keep the mountain's boulders from tumbling down.

**Solutions:** Not to many solutions to these problems. Some situations may already have a forest of trees to slow down the wind's momentum or feeling of vulnerability and exposure. Or, it may be possible to plant trees or erect a wall. Perhaps the inhabitants are away most of the day and can get their warmth and sun light elsewhere. The anxiety of being beneath a potential avalanche is not likely to be mitigated by placing a mirror to deflect the negative ch'i or using a concave mirror facing the mountain wall to make it "smaller" and less intimidating. In short, avoid living in a house that is built at the bottom of a canyon wall or under a rock overhang – avoid living in the "tiger's jaw."

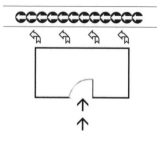

### 6. River, rain water drainage ditch or roadway directly behind the house.

River, rain water drainage ditch or a roadway directly behind the house weakens and undermines the stability of the house. Prosperity and good opportunities are easily washed away. The faster the traffic on the roadway or the swifter the flow of the river, the faster good fortune goes down stream.

**Solutions:** You can try erecting a fence or planting a hedge between your house and the fast moving road or river though these solutions are not likely to be very effective especially if the river or roadway is loud enough to be heard throughout the day. The situation is even worse, if the noise is obvious throughout the night.

The back portion of the house should be away from busy activity. Busy activities should only be at the front of the house. Activity rooms like the living room should be in the front of the house while bedrooms should be to the back so the back of the home should be quiet and the residents should not have to be disturbed by loud activities going on behind the home. Flagpoles or windsocks may work to "lift" the ch'i out of a shallow ditch while being totally ineffectual in a fast moving river.

### 7. Excessive outside noises or obnoxious smells.

We generally think of feng shui as assessing problems of structure and placement of objects in the environment. Noise and obnoxious smells in the outside environment must also be taken into consideration especially for those living in larger urban centers.

Living near an airport of any size, along heavily trafficked streets or loud factories will disturb rest, distract from work, and affect intimacy. In many situations keeping windows closed and playing music that you find appealing will mask the outside noise.

Living near a garbage dump, chemical manufacturing, sewage treatment plants, or other sources of foul smells and toxic pollutants can be quite unhealthy. Burning incense or diffusing essential oils might mask odors coming from outside. But you really need to evaluate why you are choosing to live in a basically unhealthy environment.

**Solutions:** Consider moving as soon as possible.

### 8. House too close to utility pole transformer, power generator stations or substations, cell phone microwave dish installations, airport radar, or nuclear power plant.

The question here is, "how close is too close?" Twenty-five yards is definitely too close. Even fifty yards is probably too close to a transformer can on a utility pole. One hundred yards or two hundred yards? What is too close to

a power generator station or substation? Is a mile or two miles sufficient to avoid the harmful effects of radar doppler emanations? Within fifty miles is probably too close to a nuclear power plant.

Take into consideration not just the actual physical reality of how close is too close as determined by measurement but also take into consideration the current state of your health. Do you already have various ailments specifically of the immune, hormonal or nervous systems? Or any degenerative diseases such as cancer, arteriosclerosis, heart disease, or _____ (fill in the blank)? If the answer is "yes" to any of the above health concerns then don't even think of submitting your fragile, weak body to further insult.

**Solution:** If you have been living in close proximity to any of the above sources of electro-magnetic or microwave pollution, move immediately. Find the most restful home situation, get on a good detox program, and get support from an experienced healthcare professional. And get far from harmful debilitating electro-magnetic, microwave or nuclear radiation. Filling the home with potted plants will do much to neutralize the otherwise harmful effects of the electro-magnetic, microwave or nuclear waves. But I wouldn't count on it cause the only way you would know if it works is if you don't succumb to some illness of a compromised immune system. Make the choice to live a good distance from these life diminishing situations.

*Good Luck*

~ Gathering Clues About a Home's Feng Shui ~

# Gathering Clues About a Home's Feng Shui

## The Law of the Predecessors

There's no place like home.
~~ Dorothy in "The Wizard of Oz"

It is a very ancient feng shui belief that each home has an energetic blueprint. This energetic blueprint will affect the inhabitants of a dwelling just as any container will shape whatever shapeable substance is poured into it. The Law of the Predecessors considers that the fate of previous occupants is likely to be the fate of all occupants in the future; as all occupants will ultimately be shaped by the container they are living in and subjected to the same configurations and energetic flow of ch'i.

This is also evident in how the home absorbs the vibrations of previous tenants. If there was a tragic death, that energy becomes part of the energy of the structure of that dwelling. Over the years I have met many real estate agents who concur that some homes "feel" happy and some "feel" sorrowful or that some rooms within a home may "feel" happy or sad.

It is for this reason that homes sold due to foreclosure can be assumed to be homes with unfortunate money karma. Homes sold as a result of long debilitating illness ending in a tragic or untimely death are likely to indicate homes that will adversely affect all future occupants with ill-health or early and unexpected death.

A few years ago while house hunting, my wife and I entered a home and I immediately observed feng shui indicators for difficulties in relationships. We spoke to the current tenant who was showing the home and discovered he was trying to find someone to take over the lease so he could move to a new dwelling. I encouragingly stated, "I hope you are moving to a finer home?" "No," he gloomily replied. Actually he and his wife had just divorced and he was moving to a smaller apartment. Essentially it was this experience and many others over the next four months of house hunting that led to the Feng Shui Checklist approach of this book.

### Space Clearing / House Blessings

Regardless of what you have discovered about the former residents, it is very important to do a house blessing and a land clearing. As you do the blessing and clearing, it is essential that you do it with the awareness that you are clearing out all predecessor-energy and as a way to establish your own presence. House

blessings and space clearings can be done with three sticks of incense symbolizing the Trinity, smudging with burning sage, ringing Tibetan bells, singing bowls, or sprinkling sea salt around the outside periphery of the dwelling. If you live in an apartment or attached dwelling, walk around the inside ringing your bells, cymbals or bowls, sprinkling sea salt, and making your prayers. Prayerful awareness is most important to clear negativity and attract blessings.

As you recite your prayers, remember you are "affixing" your prayer to the ever expanding smoke or sound and so your prayer expands infinitely. The sprinkling of a few grains of sea salt around the periphery illuminates a so-called energetic dome around your home as crystals refract light while the sea salt anchors your awareness of this energetic dome around your home. It is not so much for protection, as much as for establishing the parameters of your sense of personal space. You claim it, and it is yours. No other energy (i.e. thought forms) can enter your space without your permission. In this way you do not have to be warding off negativity but rather any negativity coming in your direction will detour and flow around your space and continue on elsewhere.

### Altering the Fate of a House

The Law of Predecessors states: "What has happened to previous tenants undoubtedly will happen to future occupants if the future occupants are not aware of the ability of feng shui to alter an environment." Understandably some situations cannot be altered. In "House Problems With No Remedies: Houses to Avoid" (page 27), is a list of eight situations that are either impossible to change, highly unlikely to be changed, and/or are not worth the effort to change, such as, a power transformer attached to a utility pole within 25 yards of a bedroom, or a house built on swamp land or landfill. In these situations the Law of the Predecessor will not be altered.

The majority of the remaining situations can at least be considered as potentially changeable depending on the severity of the situation. Again some may ultimately be deemed unworkable. Consider beams for example. Are they situated over beds, desks and other frequently used locations? If so, how large are they? How close or high up are they? Can they be painted, rounded or decorated away? If yes, the new inhabitants will be able to avoid the deleterious effects of living under a "weight-bearing" beam. If not, then the next tenant will suffer the same unfortunate fate as the previous tenant who "buckled" under the downward pushing pressure of the same beam.

### Same House, Different Utilization

Beside the actual configuration of the structure and its position in the surrounding environment, new tenants can utilize the interior very differ-

ently than previous tenants. Tenants whose misfortune may have been due to evasive "hidden arrows" emanating from sharp-edged furniture in proximity to the bed, desk or other areas of frequent use, from positioning their bed in direct line of the door into the bedroom, or allowing the front entrance way to become over grown and in disrepair.

And always the question has to be asked about any feng shui solution, "Is this a band-aid or a cure?" Realistically, very few homes for sale were built with an innate sense of good feng shui. Homes that are built by people applying feng shui principles are usually homes that were built for personal use and not for sale. Consequently, in lieu of actually building your own home, consider that any home you buy or rent will be flawed and will require feng shui corrections.

First, the severity of the problem needs to be determined and then the appropriate remedies need to be put in place to transform the house into a dwelling of health, harmony and prosperity. Almost every problem has an acceptable solution which is why using feng shui principles and concepts to analyze a home is so important.

One way to get some clues as to what a home has in store for you is to research, if possible, the lives of those who preceded you. Then as you continue reading the questions on the Feng Shui Checklist, look for clues in the structure of the house that may reflect eventual problems in your finances, love life, or health. But, even if the feng shui indicates there should be a problem, and no one is experiencing a problem, don't fix what isn't broken, nonetheless, watch and pay attention to future developments.

Remember, just because your predecessors may have had problems, does not mean you will. Their problems may be due to how they utilized the space. Your advantage over those who came before you is that you have the benefits of feng shui to guide you.

---

**On the Feng Shui Checklist Worksheet answer
the following questions pertaining
to the previous tenants:**

9. Were the previous owners financially successful? After this house, did they move up in life to a better situation (leave blank)? Or down ☑?
10. Did the previous owners or tenants have serious relationship problems?
11. Did the previous owners or tenants have serious health problems?
12. Did the previous owners or tenants have other major problems to consider?

# First Criteria

## Does It Meet Your Needs

**Does It Feel Right?**

Of course many homes for rent or sale that you will walk into will not have any appeal to you. This may be because of the neighborhood, the condition of the dwelling, or some unexplainable feeling that prompts you to recoil and exit without hesitation. Then there will be those that you will consider thoughtfully enough that if indeed they are contenders, you will want to put the address on the top of one of your copies of the Feng Shui Checklist and begin an examination. Unless some feature is glaringly inauspicious, save your evaluation for when you have a quiet moment alone.

**Does the House Satisfy the Basic Requirements of You & Your Family?**

However, there are often other factors that may bear on your decision making such as availability in your price range, in an area you want to live due to proximity to work, schooling, outdoor hobbies (beach, skiing, etc.) and a myriad of other motivating factors that may be totally unique to you and your needs or desires. Is it urban or rural? Do you prefer cosmopolitan or reclusive? If you need a home office, is it large enough to operate a home-base business? Is it in an area of like-minded people? Does it provide the quality of life you desire? If not, a "complaint" in the subconscious finds way to express itself and possibly undermine your health, relationship harmony, and worldly success. It is very important to evaluate your psychological relationship with where you live.

---

**On the Feng Shui Checklist Worksheet answer
the following questions pertaining
to your initial feelings and needs:**

13. Does it feel good – do you like the appearance, neighborhood, views, etc.?

14. Does it offer enough space for your (and your family's) current needs?

15. Does it offer enough space for your needs (and the needs of your family) as it grows?

16. Does it feel safe and will it provide the opportunity for peaceful, rejuvenating sleep?

17. Is it in proximity to work and marketing?

18. If there are children, is it easy for them to get to school and after school activities without adding stressful demands on the parents?

# The Ideal House Site
## Evaluating the Property

---

*...I have already spoken of those elevations of the ground
which indicate the presence of nature's breath, with its two currents of male and
female, positive and negative energy, symbolically called dragon and tiger.
The relative position and configuration of these two, the dragon and tiger, as
indicated by hills or mountains, is the most important point,
as regards the outlines and forms of the earth's surface.*
~~Ernest J. Eitel,
*Feng-Shui: the Science of Sacred Landscape in Old China*, 1st publ. 1873.

The earliest applications of feng shui are examples of common sense due to one's first hand experience of interacting with the environment. If it's cold and windy on one side of the hill, move to the side of the hill that is warm and calm. If there's no water, move closer to where the water is. And so forth.

Another important consideration in olden days was to feel safe and secure from attacking armies, thieves and wild animals. These two basic principles, ease and safety, still hold true today and dictate the essential feng shui guidelines for all housing situations. We still consider a home's desirability by the convenience of its location and, whether we are aware of it or not, by how safe we feel.

Though marauding bandits, attacking armies and wild beasts may not be a concern in a well-policed suburb or a gated-urban apartment complex, our concern about possible danger is still very real. The subconscious-emotional mind, the so-called reptilian brain, still asks the question: "What if...." and anticipates dangers like saber-toothed tigers lurking in the shadows, fears heavy objects above our heads as avalanches waiting to happen, and in the shapes all around us interpreting sharp points and edges as "arrows" headed our way. Even in the most civilized environments among our first priorities is to find safety and to feel secure.

### 19. The Armchair & the Four Celestial Animals.

Since the earliest days of feng shui practice, the ideal house site has been symbolized by an "armchair" with a high back, two arm rests and a foot stool. The high back is for support, the arm rests provide protection from the sides, and a low foot stool offers comfort and a distant view to stimulate creativity and vision.

By analogy the armchair represents the ideal for support and a view. Just as you would not sit comfortably in a chair without a high back for fear of falling backwards, in addition to the accumulated tension keeping your spine straight, so too the armchair has become a metaphor in the subconscious for support, protection and relaxation.

In ancient days this ideal house site was symbolized by the Four Celestial Animals. As children, we looked at clouds in the sky and allowed our imagination to free associate to see animal images or objects floating by. In the same way we can now use our imagination to let the forms of the landscape take the shape of animals and abstract forms. Allowing the imagination to roam freely over the landscape, we search for the Four Celestial Animals. In Chinese symbology, the Four Celestial Animals are the Black Turtle, the Azure Dragon, the White Tiger and the Red Phoenix.

The Turtle represents a mountain behind the home giving it support and protection from behind. The Turtle also literally represents "financial backing." Pointed, jagged or "broken" mountains or buildings generate anxiety keeping everyone "fired" up, restless and disjointed. On the other hand, smooth, pleasant-shaped buildings or mountains perpetuate a feeling of calm optimism and undisturbed focus.

The high-backed Dragon and the low, wide Tiger on either side energize the site and also offer their support. While the small Phoenix in front of the home, like a small footstool, allows for comfort and a distant view.

In a city environment this will equate to the size of buildings behind and on either side. If the terrain is flat and wide open in all directions or one direction or the other, the support of the Turtle behind can be symbolized by a high hedge or a few taller trees, or the Dragon or Tiger on either side can be symbolized by a fence or medium height hedge.

If you are living in an apartment building, a sculpture of a turtle or even an elephant, can be considered a "small mountain" and placed on a shelf or window sill toward the back of the apartment. Even a photograph or painting of an elephant, turtle or of a towering mountain will give the subconscious the sense of support that it needs in order to feel safe and secure.

Having a home positioned on a hillside in olden days also provided a commanding view of the valley below. Along with a mountain or hill behind a house, a house on a hillside provided a greater sense of security and has always been equated with comfort. Without security there is little, if any, rest. A body not resting experiences constant stress and anxiety. Even the

thought of an "armchair" inspires rest and relaxation. This armchair meta-phor can be used in many ways and is especially important when we evaluate the position of the bed, the desk, and even the kitchen stove.

## The Dragon's Body

Another common image used to describe the landscape made since the early days of feng shui is that of a Dragon. As we observe the undulations of mountains and valleys, we allow our imaginations to perceive the body and limbs of the Dragon. As part of this imagery, we consider the water ways of rivers, streams and brooks as representing the "veins and the blood of the Dragon" while the "breath of the Dragon" is symbolized by the wind.

Cutting into the surface of the landscape, if not done properly, can injure the "arteries and veins of the Dragon" arousing the Dragon's anger. An angry Dragon brings misfortune to those who reside in such a location. The chal-lenge of feng shui therefore is to choose the most auspicious positioning for a dwelling in relationship to the Dragon's body.

It should be obvious that a house on an exposed mountain top is equated to sitting on the "back of the Dragon." This is not a very stable position. The winds are too strong and the ch'i excessive. This unruly energy is like unruly spirits flying all over the place.

Hill top locations are locations more suited for temples and holy places, being closer to heaven and inviting to the spirit energy. Needless to say, the panoramic views are fantastic and this is often what attracts people to build in such places, and some actually do well finding a harmony uniquely suited to their particular personality. But most individuals living in such lofty, unprotected locations often suffer from nervous disorders and easily suc-cumb to escapist addictions such as alcohol or drugs in an attempt to calm down or avoid the anxiety and stresses generated in such exposed homes. In a similar manner living on the "Dragon's tail" is unstable as the tail twitches suddenly and often violently.

The best locations therefore are protected by the body and limbs of the Dragon. One of the most suitable places to site a home would be on an outcrop-ping of land extending like the "head of the Dragon" between its two limbs. Here is a commanding view while being protected from behind and on both sides.

## 20. The Green Dragon & the White Tiger in proper balance.

In order to balance the undulating energy of the Dragon, the subconscious needs the counter energy of the Tiger with its strength and mass taking the form of a hill or row of trees. As we project these images into the environment,

the natural balance is to let the more aggressive left eye perceive the more unpredictable, prowling Tiger, ready to pounce, to take shape to the left of the home (as we look at the house). In counterbalance to the Tiger, the more joyous, yet awesomely powerful Dragon is perceived with the more intimate right eye on the right side of the house (as we stand looking at it).

The Dragon on the right side of the house is referred to as the Green or Azure Dragon, while the Tiger on the left side is referred to as the White Tiger. Preferably the Dragon should be higher than the Tiger. It is said that if the Azure Dragon is higher or more dominant than the White Tiger, the White Tiger is controlled by the Dragon and remains quiet. When the Tiger is peaceful, the Dragon energy is dynamized for action. If on the other hand the White Tiger is higher or more dominant than the Azure Dragon, the Tiger becomes vicious and attacks the occupants.

In natural surroundings, a hill on the Dragon-side of the house site should be higher than the hill on the Tiger-side. If the terrain is fairly or completely flat than trees will replace the hills. If in a city environment, other homes or buildings will symbolize the Dragon and the Tiger.

This imagery repeats itself in the actual structure of the home as well. Preferably a garage should be on the Dragon-side for action allowing the Tiger to rest. If there is a second floor to the dwelling, it too should be balanced whereas if it is more to the left or right it will favor either the Dragon or the Tiger. Likewise, if the front door cannot be toward the center of the structure, again the Dragon-side would be preferable.

The Dragon is male-yang energy; the Tiger is female-yin energy. In this imagery of Dragon and Tiger we again see the necessity of balancing the yin and the yang with the Tiger symbolizing yin and the Dragon yang. A house built with a strong Tiger-side will result in a yin-yang imbalance with the woman of the house being dominant and the man struggling to assert his identity.

Some commentators say having the Dragon-side stronger is a gender issue which favors the man of the house as dominant over the female of the house. In this way it is believed the male dominant societies maintained supremacy while relegating woman to quieter and more subservient roles. This may indeed have been true in those societies where the man is the bread winner and must be given support for his public persona.

In our modern societies, where both men and women may have professional careers and active social lifestyles, this need for balance is still true.

For these men and women the Dragon still must be stronger to activate their public selves while allowing their feminine sides, symbolized by the Tiger, to enjoy the rest and intimacy desired by their personal lives. Evaluate some of your former dwellings and see how this has manifested in your life in the past and choose the balance between the Dragon and the Tiger that is right for you.

Consider the counterbalances of which side the garage is on, front door, second story, fences, hedges, next door neighboring homes or buildings. Consider in your equation any form in the environment that can be construed as a Dragon or a Tiger. Your final evaluation will describe the yin-yang balance of the inhabitants one to another.

### 21. Soil quality and greenery.

Traditionally, one major criteria for selecting a home site was the quality of the soil. It was the belief that if plant life wasn't growing on a location, the life ch'i in the ground was deficient and it wouldn't nourish the human occupants either. In fact, a feng shui practitioner without dirt under his or her nails was indicative of a feng shui practitioner who was not doing their job adequately. More experienced feng shui practitioners in olden times were able to taste the soil and determine whether it was too acidic or if it was properly alkaline.

Of course in olden days it was less likely that topsoil would be trucked in to turn a relatively harsh landscape into a verdant paradise with water piped in from thousands of miles away to be used in maintaining orchards, residential dwellings and resort hotels with lush landscaping.

Unhealthy or dying vegetation may be an indication of land that lacks vitality to support not just the vegetation, but those who dwell in a house built on the property. Patchy or barren spots, dead trees and scrawny weeds may indicate that life force is being drained from the house site. This needs to be carefully evaluated as the vegetation may just be suffering from neglect due to the lack of attention by the previous land owners. In any event dead limbs on trees, dead or dying plants should be removed immediately. But still questions need to be asked: did they neglect the landscaping due to money problems? or are they already living somewhere else and figuring maintenance of the landscape will be someone else's concern once the property is sold? Is there adequate water available for landscape maintenance?

Landscape features to avoid, change or remove if possible are trees such as the weeping willow with its droopy, weepy appearance which often reflects real sadness, pessimism or depression. Remove "hostile" thorny plants from near the front door or along the pathway to the front door. This includes members of the cactus genus, beautiful rose bushes, along with the colorful but thorny bougainvillea. I've yet to meet any home owner with bougainvillea who has not reported being repeatedly cut and scratched by these plants in their attempt to shape or maintain them. Bougainvillea and other thorny plants are best grown on property with room to grow without need of human intervention. Unless you can find thornless varieties.

In general colorful flowers are desirable. Evergreens are preferred as they stay green and represent longevity. Deciduous trees (trees that loose their leaves), especially in front of the home, are probably best avoided (if you have a choice) as they appear "dead" throughout the winter season and often feel out of place in non-wintery locations like Florida, Hawai'i and other tropical and sub-tropical locales. Hedges along with fences are an excellent way to create barriers between the home and unsightly or aggressive neighborhood factors.

### 22. Rhomboid-, trianglular-, diamond-, animal- or object-shaped property.

Square or rectangular-shaped property is the easiest to work with and provides the greatest sense of balance to the subconscious. Often land division is determined by the natural topography where rivers or other natural features dictate where to draw the line. When this occurs, many geometrical shapes other than the square and rectangle result.

Square and rectangular-shaped property is often found in cities and housing developments where streets are laid out in a grid of parallel streets. Odd-shapes can be found in housing developments especially around a cul-de-sac. Depending on the overall shape of a property under development, odd-shape lots are found in subdivisions as the real estate developers partition their property for maximum profit squeezing in houses wherever they can. Whether odd-shaped or not, avoid positioning the front door opposite an angle or having the path to the front door come from a corner of the property.

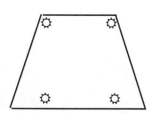

• Rhomboid: Rhomboid-shaped property comes in two basic types: the Dust Bin and the Money Bags. Some authorities say money is easily swept into a dust bin while others say a "dust bin" allows the money to easily fall out.

**Solutions:** With this in mind a "dust bin" can be modified by adding a barrier such as a hedge or fence to trap the good ch'i once it has flowed in, that is, bring in the sides to create a bit more closure.

A property shaped like a "money bag," narrow at the top and wider at the bottom, on the other hand, has no problem holding onto abundance but may have the opposite problems of attracting the good ch'i to come in through the narrow opening. This can be accomplished by installing lights, landscaping or other ch'i attracting features at the front of the property.

• Triangle: This is one of the worse shapes for a piece of property as it is difficult to site a house that will feel balanced. As with an odd-shaped house, there is a feeling of incompleteness, that something is missing.

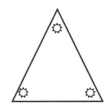

**Solutions:** The larger the triangle-shaped property is the more varied the possibilities of partitioning the land into usable shapes and the more possibilities for siting the home with a sense of harmony. Hedges or fences can be used to partition while energizers like trees or lamp posts can be installed in the corners to bring some balance while strengthening the weak corners.

• Diamond: Like the triangle, a diamond-shape makes siting a house awkward. Siting a home parallel to a back or side of the property gives a sense of proportion. Furthermore, if there are other homes nearby, the corners of a diamond-shape property will be generating "hidden arrows" that shoot out at these other homes.

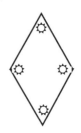

**Solutions:** Installation of lamps, flag poles and appropriate hedging and landscaping will do much to bring these awkward shapes into proportion.

• Animal shapes: Depending on the size of the property, animal shapes can be easy to work with though positioning of the home may require some creative forethought. Understandably, avoid any property that looks like a vicious animal or animal that you have a negative association with. Even if the property is shaped like an animal you like, avoid positioning the home in a less than noble part of the animal's body. Consider if the home will be in the belly or the anus. Is it being devoured by the mouth (negative) or sitting at the brow (positive)?

**Solutions:** Using landscape design of planting beds, pathways or lighting may help reconfigure an otherwise ugly shape and strengthen weak areas.

• Object shapes: Some shapes can be quite interesting and beneficial such as a money bag – small at the front and wide at the back though two lamp posts at the narrow mouth may still be required to energize the entrance. Shapes like a boot, butcher's cleaver or dust pan, like animal shapes, may require some creative forethought to determine proper positioning.

**Solutions:** Avoid negative objects. On properties that are shaped like a cleaver or a boot avoid positioning the home so it is being "booted" by the boot or "chopped" by the cleaver's blade. Place a mirror on the opposite wall to "pull" the bed back into the house.

The problem of the dust pan is that whatever comes in easily falls out. For a dust pan use hedges, trees or lamp posts to create a barrier to keep the ch'i that flows in from flowing out again.

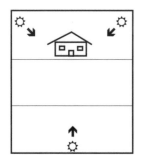

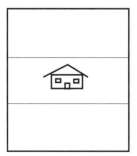

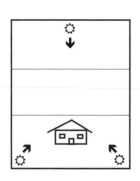

## 23. House situated on the front or back third of the property.

Some teachers associate the positioning of the house with the success of future generations. No back yard means no descendants or descendants that will receive no inheritance. A home with no back yard may also have difficulty getting opportunities that come "down the road" which may not be a problem if the family is very rich to begin with. A home situated too close to a road is often equated with quick success in life but not long lasting success as success quickly leaves. Such a home tends to be unstable.

**Solutions:** Regardless of the shape or size of the property, a home sited half way between the road and the back of the property is best. Situated on the middle third gives space between the home and the activities associated with the front of the house and its usual proximity to a road while the back of the house gives adequate space for retreat and privacy.

One of the best solutions to suggest for homes not in the middle third of the property is the proper use of outdoor lighting to energize and bring balance. The lamp posts should be installed on either side of the front or back of the house according to whichever side is smaller.

If you are too close to the road try placing trees, hedges, fences, lamp posts, water fountains to mediate. If the backyard is small, try using spotlights to lighten and enliven the backyard ch'i while pushing the house itself forward.

Using spotlights can be even more effective if they are mounted at the front or back corners of the property and aimed at the roof line. When the spotlights are turned on, they will "push" the house toward the center of the property. A third spotlight also aimed at the roof, should be positioned on the opposite side of the house to maintain a proper push-pull balance.

## 24. Houses built on top of a hill – on the "dragon's head."

Though being on the top of hill may be good protection from floods, it leaves one vulnerable to excessive winds. The excessive winds experienced by houses built on the top of a hill make it difficult to accumulate beneficial ch'i. The continuous and intense wind is constantly scattering opportunities and good fortune. The effect is lessen if the inhabitants are gone most of the day and considerably intensified for anyone home frequently with the feeling that their thoughts, ideas and brains are figuratively being "blown" all over the place. Escapist tendencies of alcohol or drug abuse are likely attempts to deal with a difficult to deal with situation (compare page 41, "Dragon's Body").

**Solutions:** Trees can be planted to slow down the effects of the wind but even so, homes in these locations tend to be in constant emotional turmoil. Constant wind encourages restlessness of the mind, increases irritability and makes it difficult, if not impossible, to rest at night, feel secure in life, and maintain emotional equilibrium.

### 25. House built too close to the ocean or body of water.

A house built too close to the ocean will continually feel the surge of the surf with the emotional waters of the human body continually surging along with it. On calm days emotions will be calm and the sea will be experienced as a "sea of tranquility." But on days of tumultuous oceanic activities, lives become filled with out-of-control melodrama and crescendos of hysteria. As the subconscious never relaxes, dream-states are also likely to be disturbed and disturbing as well.

**Solutions:** Living near any body of clean water is considered very favorable as water is symbolic of abundance including financial abundance. Facing a river, lake, pond or ocean is especially favorable. Living too close of course brings its own problems such as the risk of flooding or undermining of the home's foundation. How close is too close is once again a question that requires careful consideration. It would be much better to live on a hillside looking out toward the ocean which appears calm, placid and which will be creatively inspiring.

### 26. Mountain or large building over-poweringly close behind or on either side of the home.

You do not want a huge mountain or skyscraper towering directly behind your home. This will feel oppressive in a way that will weaken the inhabitants and lead to feelings of depression and despair. Back problems are also likely as you attempt to "hold back" that heavy weight. This may be too difficult to alter depending on the size of the mountain and how close to the house it is. Huge buildings on either side of a house also feel oppressive to those living in smaller dwellings.

**Solutions:** You can try a concave mirror to diminish the size of the over-powering building(s) or mountain(s) but this may only be a temporary solution.

### 27. Home located at the end of a dead-end street or a cul-de-sac.

Locating a home on the end of a dead-end street symbolizes that one's life has "no where else to go." Ideally, ch'i flows toward our home on roadways like a river bringing opportunity and good fortune. Our challenge is to accumulate some of this life-giving ch'i for our benefit but then to let it circulate away from us before it becomes stagnant, unhealthy and unfortunate. Many dead-end streets are too narrow for the energy to circulate.

A cul-de-sac, like a dead-end street, also symbolizes the end of the road. However, unlike a dead-end street that comes to an abrupt stop, a cul-de-sac usually comes to an end that is wide like a full sack. The end of a cul-de-sac allows cars to make a complete turn. Also, instead of one house at the very end of the street receiving all the dead-end energy of the road that abruptly stops, there are usually a few homes situated all along the end of the cul-de-

"Dead-end, cul-de-sac. The names say it all. Nowhere to go."

~~ James A. Moser

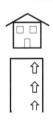

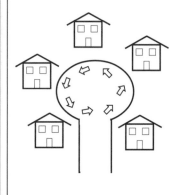

sac – all of which get "sliced" by the cars, or the road itself, as it turns in front of them.

One problem with a cul-de-sac is there is no where to go but back the way you came so ch'i stagnates. Another problem is the "hidden arrows" of the cars (or the roadway itself even when there are no cars) which "cuts" into the homes lined up along the end of the sack. For similar reasons it is better to build your house on the inside bend of a river or roadway to be embraced rather than on the outer edge where your home will be sliced (see #28 below). The outside bend of a river is always more heavily eroded as the water sweeps by. A faster moving river or road intensifies the destruction and adds to the emotional turbulence of the inhabitant's lives.

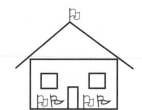

**Solutions:** If the dead-end street comes to a wide open field with far reaching views, or is wide enough to allow cars to make a complete turn, this may change our evaluation. One suggested cure is to mount a large mirror at the end of the road to reflect the roadway approaching it and to create the illusion that the roadway "continues on."

If the cul-de-sac is wide enough, the residents of this cul-de-sac could construct a traffic circle in the center to allow the ch'i to flow in and out while further energizing the area with a bubbling fountain in the center surrounded by flowers and pleasant foliage. With a circle in the center the configuration is no longer a cul-de-sac but becomes a "keyhole" instead. In addition each home along the curve of the cul-de-sac could mount an oval or eight-sided mirror to deflect the attacking "hidden arrows" as well as put up fences and plant hedges as a protective barrier.

Evaluate each cul-de-sac according to how it feels – wide or narrow, slightly elevated, top of a steep hill, end of downhill, neighboring houses jammed close together or homes separated to allow pleasant distant views. Consider also if there is an "exit" through a backyard for security. As Grandmaster Yap Cheng Hai commented, "the problem with a cul-de-sac is that there is no exit in case of fire or danger. I have a gate in my back yard so if there is an emergency, I can walk out into the neighboring meadow."

Keeping the ch'i flowing in without getting stagnant is another primary concern of those living on a cul-de-sac. If the ch'i comes flowing in and has no where to go, it stagnates as fresh ch'i has no way of getting in, consequently, those living on a cul-de-sac likewise become stagnant in their lives with a feeling of "going no where" in a relationship or a career. The challenge of the cul-de-sac is to keep the ch'i flowing and this can be done with whirligigs, wind socks, wind chimes, weather vanes, banners and even small windmills.

**28. Home located on outer edge of a river, roadway or freeway overpass.**

Finding a choice location to live in a large city laced with freeways and large thoroughfares is often difficult. If you leave every morning for work and

do not come home until evening, the noise level from busy, fast-moving roadways may not be overwhelming, especially if the roadway quiets down during the evening hours and you can enjoy your evening meal and sleep in restful quiet. I am sure it most be equally difficult to maintain peace of mind and family harmony living in close proximity to railroad tracks with trains rumbling by at regular intervals.

**Solutions:** To mask the sound of outside noise, music can be played that is appropriate for the occasion. However, if it is impossible to drown out the outside noise seriously consider living somewhere else.

If you are house hunting, and you visit a house that you really consider a potential candidate for your next home and it happens to be a week-end or holiday, be sure to go back during the week to get a true appreciation of the neighborhood noise levels especially during rush hour. If you work at home, neighborhood noise will be of a greater concern, so evaluate this one carefully. Also consider that the closer you are to roadway noise, the closer you are to automotive emissions, dirt and debris. Remember choosing a home is also choosing a healthy life-style.

### 29. From the front door you can see the road coming to the home and then going away.

Do you "see money coming and going?" Roadways are symbolic rivers and like rivers, roads bring commerce and prosperity as a link to the rest of the world. But like a fast moving river, a busy trafficked street can also take money and opportunity away. There is also the additional problem of "hidden arrows" shooting at the home as cars come towards the house.

**Solutions:** Some authorities differentiate between a river/road that comes from the left going to the right or one coming from the right and going to the left. Going to the right brings abundance while going left takes it away. Especially if the river, road or drainage ditch is behind the house (page 30, #6).

Ideally, a home should be embraced by a river/road with ch'i/money/ opportunity coming to you where you can leisurely and comfortably reach out and take some. In contrast, being on the outside of the river, though you see it coming, you also see it leaving. The challenge is to draw the good ch'i flowing your way – to eddy up to your home where it can accumulate. This can be done with hedges, driveway lights and planting flowers along the driveways and walk ways to the front entrance. Planting hedges or erecting fences can also be installed to protect the house from the "hidden arrows" shooting at the house by cars driving towards the home from either direction. But in most situations, this an inadequate solution but certainly worth a try.

One of the oldest feng shui textbooks, the Water Dragon Classic, provides many formulas used to determine the best direction for water to flow to and

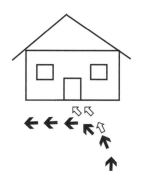

The amount of chi flowing and whether it accumulates or is rapidly dispersed at any particular point, is the crux of feng-shui. An auspicious site or hsueh (dragon's lair) needs to be near a good strong flow of chi, but not necessarily on the main vein or artery, which may even carry away its beneficent influences almost as fast as it brings them!

~~ Stephen Skinner, *The Living Earth Manual of Feng-Shui: Chinese Geomancy*

away from a home. To apply these formulas requires more than just a beginner's knowledge of feng shui theory and application.

### 30. "Tiger eyes" in the night.

"Tiger eyes" in the night refers to the headlights of on-coming traffic. Observing a potential dwelling by daylight may not reveal that at night time, the headlights of cars, which could be on a roadway somewhat distant from the home, are "shooting" their piercing beams into one or more of the living areas of the home. To make the situation worse if the home is close to heavily trafficked roads, in addition to the beams of light flickering across your room(s), there will also be the continuous noise of cars clipping along the road surface.

**Solutions:** If there are "tiger eyes" piercing a home, try to determine if a hedge or fence can be put into place to shield you from this aggressive disturbance.

### 31. Parking a car pointing directly at the front door, bedroom or other frequently used room.

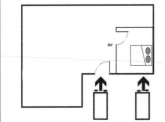

Parking a car directly in front of the front door is the equivalent of parking a car in your mouth as the front door is the "mouth of ch'i". Cars, when they stop, "shoot arrows" straight ahead. Consequently, when cars pull up in a carport or parking area in front of a home, they shoot their "arrows" straight ahead. It is for this same reason you do not want to pull up outside of someone's bedroom or "attack" the entrance doorway. Even when the cars are not pulling in or out they will be felt as if they are.

**Solutions:** If another parking area can not be found, try to angle your vehicles so they do not point directly at the house itself. It's okay if the room(s) closest to the road or parking area is a utility room or bathroom as a buffer or if the parking area is along side of house with no rooms receiving the killing-ch'i. And whatever you do, do not back up into a garage if the garage is connected by a doorway to the main part of the house as this forces the gas emissions under the door and into the house both when leaving and when returning. This habit is even worse if the door leads into a kitchen or other frequently used room.

### 32. Business or home located at a T-section, Y-section or busy corner lot.

Properties located on the outside bend of a road or even on a corner lot usually experience misfortune in health, relationship and overall prosperity. The problem in all of these situations is the constant disturbance of the ch'i that results from cars braking, stopping and accelerating again.

This is made even worse at a T-section as the cars coming down the roadway toward the building are shooting "hidden arrows" at the inhabitants as

well as creating disturbance by braking, stopping and accelerating again. The situation is even worse if the front door itself and the pathway to the front door are in direct alignment with the on-coming traffic.

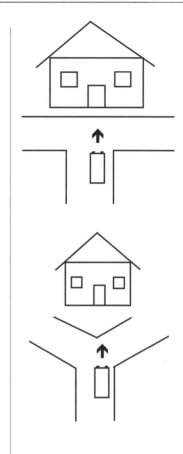

**Solutions:** The best that can be done in this most undesirable situation is to plant hedges and erect fences. A hedge, fence or, even better, a solid wall should be several feet high. It is also a good idea to mount an eight-sided Ba-gua mirror to face the direction of the on-coming vehicles and will also protect the house from constantly being blasted by bright headlights, "tiger's eyes" in the night (page 50, #30). At least reposition the pathway and hope that a hedge, fence and Ba-gua mirror is adequate for protecting the front door as well as the house in general.

Deciding if these solutions are at best like band-aids on a gaping wound depends on the busyness of the street. Occasional cars headed your way will be less harmful. Constant traffic in addition to the energy shooting at the home also adds distracting automotive noise plus noxious gas emissions. But realize, even without vehicular traffic, the roadway itself is an "arrow" shooting at the house. Another suggested method of deflecting the "hidden arrows" of the roadway is to erect a small windmill to disperse the killing ch'i.

### 33. House on the road without a curb or step up to the front door.

The problem of a home situated at street level without a curb or step up to the front door is the home can easily be flooded literally by actual water run-of after a heavy rain, and figuratively "flooded" even when it is not raining.

**Solutions:** Add a curb to channel real rivulets of rain water away from the front door if it were to rain. In additon this will give security to the emotional concern of "what if it does rain" even when it is not. It would also be helpful to use up-lighting, put the house numbers above the door way, hang a pleasant sounding wind chime or colorful windsock to "lift" the ch'i.

### 34. House or apartment situated below street level.

The problem of a home situated below street level without a curb or step up to the front door is an even more vulnerable situation then being at street level without a curb or step up to the front door. Not only is there worry about what if it rains but what if something drives off the street and through the window. A general sense of anxiety also pervades due to a fear of invasion from above.

**Solutions:** In addition to a curb to channel rainwater away from the home consider a hedge or fence to provide a feeling of protection from the possibly out-of-control activity of the roadway. Out of sight, out of mind may apply in this situation. To "lift" the ch'i of the home place the numbers above the door and

use up-lighting. Hanging flower baskets, wind chimes or wind socks can also be effective. Most of all avoid further "burying" the home with hedges or fences, or in any way hide the entrance way.

### 35. House below a roadway.

A house below a roadway is similar to a home situated below a river or lake. Eventually the house gets "flooded." In this case the house gets flooded by the roadway energy which includes gas fumes and noise, especially if it is a frequently traveled roadway. The worst possible situations are where the house is at the bottom of the driveway receiving the "killing" energy of the cars, real or imaginary traveling up and down. This will also be negatively experienced during heavy rains when the rainwater pours down the driveway and floods the garage or house itself.

**Solutions:** At least make sure there are drainage ditches to properly channel the rainwater away. Position a small eight-sided mirror to deflect the "hidden arrows" produced by any cars coming down the hill toward the house. Planting tall trees or installing flagpoles, weather vanes, or even spotlights on the ground aimed up to the roof line. All these devices can help "lift" the ch'i of a home and thereby lift the spirits of the inhabitants promoting confidence, enthusiasm, optimism and creative thinking.

### 36. House at the bottom of a steep driveway or hill – an "uphill struggle."

In addition to the possible flooding factor during heavy rains there is the difficult experience of getting up the driveway. The effort needed to accelerate comes to represent effort and obstruction in other areas of life or a constant "uphill struggle." This is even more blatant if the car lacks power and you have to press down hard on the accelerator in your attempt to "get up that hill." This negative influence may be increased the longer and/or the narrower the driveway actually is. The increased sense of insecurity accelerating up a long narrow driveway can certainly add to the stress of getting up that hill. On the other hand, the negative impact of "struggling uphill" will be lessened if you remain home most of the time and do not have to make an effort to go to work each day.

**Solutions:** A helpful solution to counter the "life-is-an-uphill-struggle" scenario, that is to mitigate the stress-filled struggle to get to the top of the driveway, is a lush and varied landscaping. A nicely landscaped driveway serves to pull the driver upward like tying knots in a large rope to assist the climber in getting to the top. The mind in this case is distracted by the variety and the beauty of the landscaping and is entertained on the way up lessening, and perhaps even canceling, the negative impact of the effort. A wide and nicely paved driveway enhances the effect of a pleasant drive to the

top. Flagpoles, weather vanes, windmills and spotlights can all be used with effectiveness.

### 37. House at the top of a steep road or driveway – "opportunities roll away."

Houses at the top of a steep road or driveway experience an "uphill struggle" to get home; and even with the emergency brake and wheels turned to the curb, will feel tense and uncertain especially when that emergency brake is pulled to its maximum. Even if you have a garage to pull into, the stress will linger.

Roadways like rivers are needed to bring opportunity our way. If it moves too fast, we can't hold on to it. If we are up a hill, opportunity certainly will not easily flow up to us. In fact, perched on top of a steep incline allows the good ch'i (money and opportunities) to flow away.

It is important to evaluate other features of a home situated at the top of a steep driveway. If there is a garage, is parking the car an easy or difficult task relative to the steep roadway?  Is there at least a level lawn area between the street and the home to assist in gathering energy with foliage and lighting to catch the eye? Answer these questions carefully.

If the house and view are that wonderful and this was the only indicator of difficulty with career and financial success, I would probably take the chance especially if there is a level lawn. A steep lawn and difficult garage entrance, on the other hand, may sway me to avoid this house.

**Solutions:** Whether the hill is in front or behind a home, positioning spotlights on the down slope pointing at the roof line may be sufficient for bringing good ch'i back to you. The spotlights need to be turned on once to establish the intention that as ch'i flows away, it returns to you once again.

Once you've installed the lights they need to be turned on from time-to-time to reaffirm this intention in the subconscious and of course they can be used at other times to illuminate the home for special occasions and parties. Tall flagpoles along the downhill perimeter with bright colored banners can also be used by themselves if spotlights can not be installed.

Another solution for keeping a home's energy from rolling back down the hill is erecting two stone or brick pillars on either side of the driveway, or some other structure, that gives the feeling of containment. Hanging wind chimes on the four corners can also do much for "lifting" the home's ch'i.

### 38. House on a one-way street.

On a one-way street ch'i flows fast. Houses on a one-way street receive less opportunity than homes with traffic flowing in both directions. Roadways that allow for ch'i flow in both directions can bring opportunity from both directions.

**Solutions:** The challenge here is to slow the ch'i flow down. Narrow, meandering one-way streets such as in small European towns very naturally slow the ch'i flow down. On larger two, three or more lane one-way streets the speed of the road parallels the hyperactivity of those who live along the road. On a fast and wide one-way street uncertainty, lack of stability, striving, and struggling are the norm. There's a tendency to be ever vigilant and prepared for the unexpected and to be quick to grab an opportunity before it gets "sucked" back into the fast moving stream once again.

### 39. High walls or foliage.

High walls or foliage which make it impossible to see the roof of the house from the street makes the inhabitants feel invisible. A house with high walls or foliage that can not be seen from the street is a house that is "imprisoned."

On the one hand, a high wall or foliage provides privacy and in many cases buffers out street or even city noise. High walls or foliage can also give psychic protection to those who are insecure or afraid of being "out" in the world. But ultimately, people living in a house surrounded by high walls or foliage will feel suffocated as positive life-giving ch'i cannot get in; and whatever ch'i is already in, will become stagnant. It is only a question of time before the residents begin to suffer from a list of seemingly insurmountable problems such as, pessimism, depression, difficult to heal ailments, and increasing financial woes.

The intensity of problems increases for any resident that is home most of the day. Those who leave for work, travel or play are more likely to feel that they are coming back to a retreat instead of being "trapped" in a prison. What is "home, sweet home" for one resident may seem isolating and alienating to another.

**Solutions:** If the house is surrounded by an insurmountable wall, and the wall can not easily be reduced in its height, perhaps a flag pole can be mounted on the roof or elsewhere on the property to "flag down" the ch'i while reaching out into the world. If the house is surrounded by a high edge, the solution is easy – trim the hedge. If the hedge or wall is to be lowered, they should be lowered so that at least the eaves can be seen from the street while continuing to be high enough to maintain privacy from the unwanted gaze of passerbys and still deflect some of the street noise.

### 40. Frequently used rooms facing predominantly west.

The sun rising in the east is favorable for morning activities as the sun awakens and energizes. The sun setting however casts a different light. The light of the sun at the end of the day has more glare. An office, kitchen or other work space that requires focus and concentration will be most affected by this undesirable late afternoon glare.

**Solutions:** The solution should be easy – move your work into a different room if you can or close the curtains. It has always been a surprise to me how many homes do not have some kind of window treatment. Curtains dress up the basic structure. Ideally they should soften a room for intimacy as well as provide the option for closure. Curtains are needed most of all to protect the eyes from the glare of the setting sun in any activity room facing west where focus and concentration are required such as kitchen or home office. It is an investment that will be well worth it in work comfort, minimized eye strain and resultant productivity. If you need to be in a west facing room, at least hang a lead-glass crystal sphere in the window to fill the room with rainbows.

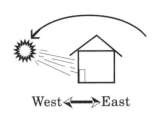

West ⟷ East

### 41. Frequently used rooms facing predominantly north.

From personal experience I can assure you that a house or an apartment that faces predominantly north is going to feel like a refrigerator in winter. Of course a north facing home will be a pleasantly cool dwelling during the hottest of summers. However, during fall through late spring, expect to bundle up or spend more money on heating bills.

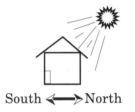

South ⟷ North

Solutions: In addition to using central heating, space heaters or layered clothing to keep warm, keep lights on to illuminate the space to avoid a cave-like feeling of isolation and forsakenness. A north facing dwelling is even more undesirable the further north you journey.

### 42. A pond in the back yard or to the left of the front door.

Having a pond on a property is considered very fortunate provided the pond is well kept. As long as the water is clean, a pond will bring good fortune as, once again, water symbolizes money or currency. Stocking a pond with fish generates even more currency. Obversely, a pond with dirty water represents "dirty money." Besides, stagnant water can be a breeding ground for bacterium, mosquitos, and algae. Stagnant water can also represent "clouded" reasoning, a sluggish body and stagnant prosperity.

Though ponds in general are fortunate anywhere on a property, there are some locations that are considered better than others. The least favorable location is behind the house where it can weaken the support of a home referred to as the Turtle in the previous discussion of the four Celestial Animals (page 39, #19).

Some say ponds should be installed only in front of the house and preferable to the right side of the entrance way as you look out. Some consider ponds positioned to the left of the home (as you look out) as an indication of eventual marital problems. Ponds in the backyard can be too yin if positioned too close to the back door of the home where they may drain finances and good health.

**Solutions:** If there is a pond, it is very important to keep it full of fresh water. If there are to be fish in the pond, choose an odd number. Consider also choosing the right water plants such as lotus, water lily or water hyacinth to create a low maintenance eco-system. With a little research it should be possible to have the right ecologically balanced arrangement of fish and water plants to keep from becoming a breeding place for bacterium, mosquitos, and algae growth.

If there is a view from your window or property of a stagnant pond that cannot be cleaned and drained by you or won't be maintained by its owners, then it is necessary for you to block it from view with a hedge or fence. On the other hand, if there is any body of water within view of your home, install a mirror to reflect it into the house for increased prosperity.

Symbolic ponds, lakes or rivers can also bring good fortune. A very large flat grassy area whether a lawn, neighboring park, or wide-open meadow in front of the home all have the benefit of bringing financial prosperity.

### 43. Swimming pools.

Swimming pools are usually installed behind a home in the backyard or behind a front fence along the side of the house. Swimming pools are meant for recreation but can bring problems as well if they are not properly placed and configured. Above ground pools should never be very close to a house as the quantity of water will be felt as "flooding" into the home in addition to the enormous amount of yin energy it contains.

If the pool is square, the corners are considered "hidden arrows" and should not point at the house so that those in bedrooms, home offices or other frequently used rooms feel they are being "shot" at.

**Solutions:** In-ground swimming pools that are kidney-shaped embracing a home are considered best. In most situations one or more potted plants can be positioned at the offensive corners of rectangular swimming pools to ameliorate their harmful influence. Also adding wood of any kind such as a fence, bushes or trees near and around the pool will help absorb the negative effects of excessive water.

A swimming pool should always be filled with water even in winter time to attract abundance. If it is deemed more appropriate to empty, put a pool cover over it so finances will not go "down the drain."

A broken or unused pool is to be avoided. If you cannot fix it, fill it in with earth before health and prosperity are "drained" away. Never allow water to become stagnant in ponds, pools, spas, cisterns or bird baths.

# Neighbors - Harmony In The Community
## Evaluating the Effect Other Homes May Have on Each Other

If there is harmony in the home,
there will be order in the nation.
If there is order in the nation,
there will be peace in the world.
~~Anonymous

Roadways, roof lines, the edges of a building, the direction of pathways, driveways, and even the fencing around a neighboring property can have a detrimental influence if they point or "shoot" directly at another dwelling. With this in mind, you do not want to live in a dwelling where roadways, pathways, driveways, and fence lines "shoot" directly at you, especially not at the front door or any of the major rooms such as kitchen, dining room, bedrooms and home office. The best solution in any of these situations is to hang potted plants or wind chimes. To ensure harmony between respective dwellings plant hedges or erect fences to protect you and them from possible "hidden arrow."

One of the most obvious mistakes made in residential neighborhoods, and in commercial areas with large office buildings, is large structures constructed among smaller ones. Take the case of the Bank of Hong Kong & Shanghai building being attacked by the Bank of China building for example. Before China reclaimed Hong Kong from the British in 1999, they built the towering Bank of China building. Not only is the Bank of China building considerably higher and therefore more dominant than the smaller Bank of Hong Kong & Shanghai building in the lower right of the picture, but notice how the edge of the bank appears as a knife "slicing through" the British Governor's Mansion situated in the lower center. After many people working in these building got ill or had accidents, the old Governor's mansion is now used only for storage.

Photo from Issue #22, Feb. 2000 by permission from "Feng Shui for Modern Living" Magazine, (currently not in circulation).

When a new high rise, subdivision or strip mall is constructed, the ch'i flow of the environment changes considerably, possibly for the better but usually for the worse. New urban developments bring urban congestion, increased air and noise pollution, and "hidden arrows" from the newly constructed wall angles and roof lines shooting in all directions. In many cases, previously built smaller one and two-story residential homes are now overshadowed and energetically squashed by the new larger structures which can be several stories high or even skyscrapers. Hopefully, cures can be installed to block or deflect these "hidden arrows."

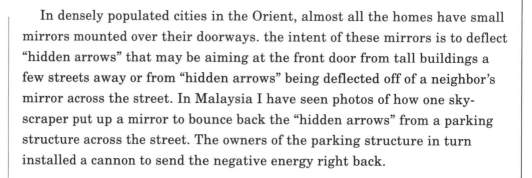

In densely populated cities in the Orient, almost all the homes have small mirrors mounted over their doorways. the intent of these mirrors is to deflect "hidden arrows" that may be aiming at the front door from tall buildings a few streets away or from "hidden arrows" being deflected off of a neighbor's mirror across the street. In Malaysia I have seen photos of how one skyscraper put up a mirror to bounce back the "hidden arrows" from a parking structure across the street. The owners of the parking structure in turn installed a cannon to send the negative energy right back.

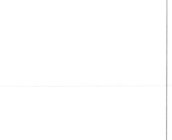

A note about the Ba-gua Mirrors sometimes sold as "feng shui mirrors." These are eight-sided mirrors which are usually red, green with eight sets of gold lines in various combinations of long lines (yang) and two short lines (yin) which are called Trigrams. These Ba-gua mirrors should never be hung inside a house and are most specifically used to "bounce" ghosts and unsettled spirit energy away from the home while drawing auspicious energy inward. Some people will use them to bounce any negative energy away. Most important of all do not hang one in your home. And if you do hang one on the outside of your house, try to angle it so you do not bounce negative energy at the home of your neighbor. Any un-framed, oval or eight-sided mirror, concave, convex or flat will be as effective as a Ba-gua Mirror in deflecting negative energy headed your way.

## 44. Neighboring roof lines, roof top antennas, fence lines, trees and hedges.

In areas where there are many homes clustered together, it is important to observe the relationship of one house to another. You should especially observe driveways, pathways, fences, landscaping, roof lines and the corners of structures.

The most obvious consideration is the relationship of one structure to another. In the past we have laughed at the "ticky-tacky" line up of homes in a housing tract – boring and conducive to conformity. How wonderful it is to be a land owner, having the freedom to design and place a home in accordance to one's own individuality and desire. Yet this freedom can unintentionally lead to community disharmony in regard to position of the structure itself and even choice of landscaping. Often I see a complete disregard as to how a newly built structure may impact a neighbor's life or the life of the inhabitants of the newly built structure for that matter.

One problem that I often observe is the misalignment of one structure with another whether from one property to another, or two structures on the same property. Simply stated, when the corner of one structure points at another structure, there will be discord between the occupants of those structures as the "hidden arrows" fly.

**Solutions:** The feng shui cure for this problem is to plant a hedge or erect a fence that is high enough to protect the house from any "arrows" pointing at

it. In addition, it would be wise to hang a metal tubular wind chime to symbolize harmony between the two structures. Other gestures can be placement of fountains or garden statuary.

### 45. Front door consumed by a "tiger's mouth."

The "tiger's mouth" refers to a larger front entrance of another structure situated opposite your front entrance way. This gives the appearance of your home being "consumed" by the opposing structure. In all likelihood if the opposing structure has a larger entrance way than your home, the structure is likely to also be more imposing, symbolic of a high mountain to climb or a great obstacle to surmount. Some say to mount a concave mirror to reflect a miniaturized image of the larger structure thus "shrinking" its negative implications of overpowering, squashing, draining, etc.

**Solutions:** If it is just the opposing doorway that is larger than yours, planting a hedge or erecting a fence to block your view as you come out of your front door should be sufficient. If the opposing edifice also towers above you then you will internalize its presence as insurmountable even if you aren't consumed by the "tiger's mouth."

### 46. Neighbor's driveway & garage door opposite your front door.

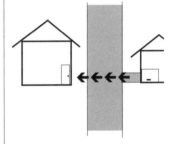

When a neighbor's driveway is opposite the front door of your house, the "killing ch'i" of their car backing out toward your home is considered unfavorable. Even their garage door opening can feel like the jaws of a monster, or "tiger's mouth." If the garage door opposite your home is opposite your garage door, equilibrium is maintained and no further action need be taken.

**Solutions:** If the garage door across the street is opposite your front door not much else can be done but to hang a small oval or eight-sided mirror on the wall of your house opposite the garage door across the street, being careful not to deflect the negative ch'i at another neighbor's front door.

### 47. House uphill from another on the same property.

The problem of owning two houses with your main residence being downhill from a rental, in-law's, children's, servant's or gardener's home is that the uphill house will tend to "lord" it over the house below it. Those living in the uphill house will act as if they own the property. It may appear that the renter or caretaker acts as if they are the owners and will try to control what goes on. They may even remain in their house after you, or any owner, sells the property and takes up residence elsewhere.

**Solutions:** To remedy this situation, the property owners should take their photograph, perhaps laminating it, then hang it somewhere further up

toward the property line on a fence or tree, or even tack it to the back wall of the uppermost structure. Doing this in effect puts the true owners in control by putting them symbolically higher on the hill. Having more authority in one's voice polarizes others not in authority not to presume they can preempt yours.

### 48. Neighbor's house higher up the hill.

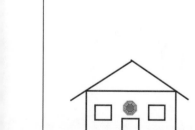

Another problem is found when one structure is higher up the hill on a different property than another. Again a tendency to discord as the inhabitants higher up will try to, and probably will succeed, in "lording" it over the inhabitants of the lower structure. This will take the form of the inhabitants of the house higher on the hill complaining continuously about what the inhabitants lower on the hill are or are not doing to their liking.

**Solutions:** To encourage harmony between the lower structure and the one up the hill consider hanging potted plants from the eaves of the roof, perhaps a sweet sounding wind chime, or even installing a pleasant sounding water fountain. However, if you do have to choose a house on a hillside street, choose a house on the side of the street with the uphill house representing the Dragon to the right (as you look at the house). If the house to the left is higher, the Tiger is strengthened and will be more difficult to bring into harmony.

### 49. Disagreeable or disturbing neighbors.

It is always unfortunate to live next to rowdy, hysterical, messy, or otherwise disagreeable people.

**Solutions:** Mirrors can also be used to deflect negative energy from a disagreeable neighbor. Beside freeing you of some of the impact, it actually might drive them away in their attempt to avoid having to deal with their own negative energy coming back at them.

### 50. Living opposite a house of worship, cemetery, hospital, mortuary, crematorium, or slaughter house.

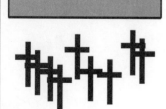

Though houses of worship can also be places for joyous celebrations, they are also associated with suffering and death. Suffering, death and decay are even more likely to be associated with cemeteries, hospitals, mortuaries, crematoriums and slaughter houses. Living opposite a cemetery, hospital, mortuary, crematorium or slaughter house is especially inauspicious as it is believed that the "spirits of the dead," pleasant or unpleasant, are attracted to such locations and eventually will exert an undermining influence on nearby residents.

Large empty structures that remain empty for long periods of time are considered very yin. Some individuals living next to large empty structures may be more vulnerable to feeling a "dampening" of their own spirits as they resonant with the "emptiness" in the structure next to their own.

**Solutions:** Hang a red, green and gold Ba-gua mirror to deflect any ghost-like energy. Say prayers that assist those of the spirit-world to know your true intent. Perhaps put guardians in the yard such as a pair of dragon-headed Fu dogs, the mythical Chinese one-horned animal call a Kirin, or concrete lions.

### 51. Living in view of a crucifix, smoke stack or other unnatural construction.

Living in view of a crucifixion on top of local churches, or even in view of factory smoke stacks is undesirable. Like electrical line and telephone poles, they are considered aggressive and attacking to the inhabitants of the dwelling.

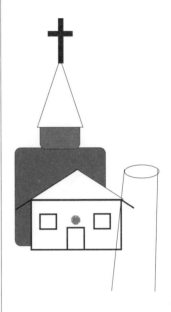

**Solutions:** Some high tension wires and utility poles look like a centipede. As a rooster feeds on centipedes, facing a statue or figurine of a rooster in the direction of the "centipede" will destroy its negative effects. Though it is best to avoid these images in the landscape, at least block them with trees, hedges or fences, or hang a red, green and gold Ba-gua Mirror to deflect any negative energy that might be coming your way.

*Stylized Chinese Character for Longevity*

*Section II*

# Interior Harmony

## The Importance of Good Ch'i Flow

Moderation and enhancement of ch'i flow

is the underlying aim of feng shui. Good ch'i flow

in a dwelling improves the ch'i of residents.

The concept of ch'i is essential for evaluating any house,

office, or plot of land, and all their internal and external elements.

Feng shui experts act like doctors of environmental ills,

discerning ch'i circulation and pulse.

They seek to create smooth, balanced, and fluid surroundings.

For example, if three or more doors or windows are aligned in a row,

they will funnel ch'i too quickly. A strategically hung wind chime

will moderate ch'i flow. On the other hand you should look out for the oppressive,

constrained ch'i of a dark and narrow hall,

which may depress and inhibit the occupant's chances

for success in life and in work.

Proper use of lights and mirrors will symbolically

open up the space.

~~ Sarah Rossbach,

*Interior Design With Feng Shui*

Choose the Best Home for You ~ The Feng Shui Checklist™

Great Good Fortune

# House Structure

## How Energy Flows Through the Home

Free-flowing ch'i is like a river
stocked with the gifts of long life, prosperity, and health.
Make sure there is plentiful ch'i that flows freely through your space.
It will bring you every rich treasure you deserve.

~~ Angel Thompson,
The Feng Shui Anthology: Contemporary Earth Design, edited by Jami Lin

It is of great importance that once the ch'i enters the home it can freely circulate through all the rooms of the home. Evaluating how the ch'i flows from room-to-room can be difficult to determine without training. Nevertheless, using intuition and some of the guidelines already mentioned should assist you in making a proper evaluation. Looking first at the floor plan and then proceeding to walk through the house beginning at the front door should give you a good indication as to how the ch'i flows by observing where walls become blockades to navigate around, which rooms seem to pull the ch'i into them, which angles feel hostile, and where ch'i gets stagnant due to lack of circulation.

There are many minor ch'i adjustments that can be made to facilitate the circulation of ch'i. There are ways to slow it down if it is moving too fast, stir it up if it is stagnant, quiet it down if it is excessive, lift it up if it is oppressive, sort it out if it is clashing, and so forth. Then consider what you may need to do to get the ch'i flowing: will a mirror "bounce" it around a corner? a mobile "stir up" a lifeless corner? or will a lead-glass crystal sphere add "sparkle?" and so on. Following are some examples of how ch'i moves through the home and the solutions to the various problems that arise.

### 52. Odd-Shape Houses - U-shape, L-shape (cleaver, boot), modular, etc.

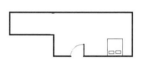

A square or rectangular-shape symbolizes the earth and psychologically represents stability, dependability and security. It is easy to control, and visually its symmetry is easy to feel in control of.

It is also important to evaluate the appearance of a house that is not square or rectangular. Does it have an animal-shape? Does the animal appear to be biting? or is the animal friendly? If the shape is missing a corner, does it look like a cleaver with a bedroom on the cutting edge? Ouch! Needless to say, positioning a bedroom on the cleaver's blade does not bode well. If there is an important room on the boot or cleaver's blade place a mirror on the opposite wall to draw the bed or desk or whatever is on the boot or the blade across the room back into the house.

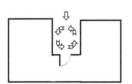

To balance an L-shaped house the usual suggestion is to install a lamp post. a flag pole or plant a tree where the missing corner of the square or rectangle would be. Filling the area in with foliage or a nicely arranged outdoor patio what also give the feeling of completeness to the shape.

A U-shaped house is not favorable as "wind" can get trapped and symbolizes turbulence. Much as the wind on a windy day blows newspapers and other debris around and around in a doorway recessed off a city street. The best solution is to remodel that portion of the house with a solid outer wall. If remodeling is not feasible, consider a gated fence or wall that is either solid wood, brick or stucco. A U-shape house is missing one of the sides with the corners intact. In a U-shaped house it is easy to feel divided within or divided from the other members of the family. It could adversely effect career success if the top of the U is the front of the house.

Needless to say, some homes are really oddly shaped and present an even greater challenge. If you can't afford to remodel, consider living somewhere else. In general, odd-shaped houses lack a "center" or a feeling of regularity and dependability. It is sometimes easy to balance a home with landscaping and placement of outdoor lights. In these situations you need to determine what cures would be necessary to remedy the situation, how difficult are they to implement, and are they worth the expense and trouble?

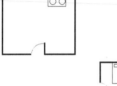

Modular houses with a master bedroom detached from the main area of the house tend to foster separation. Being detached from the kitchen and prime living area, inclines the relationship to also become separated. It is best to have the master bedroom and main living area connected. Children's rooms, home offices, family rooms, etc. do just fine when "floating" out on their own.

**Solutions:** A roofed-over walkway would be suitable solution for connecting the modular bedroom with the main part of the home. Perhaps adding a border of flowers or even a railing will strengthen the connection between modular structures.

### 53. Center of house with a fireplace, stairway or bathroom.

In many ways the center of the home represents the core or "heart" of the home. Whatever goes on at this location will directly effect the health of everyone living there.

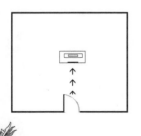

• **Fireplace:** A fireplace has both a flue and the fire burning within. Even without a fire burning, a fireplace represents a "firing up" of the adrenals. At first this helps everyone to race around accomplishing much. But in due time, and according to age and constitution of each individual, a fireplace in the center of the house will result in everyone feeling exhausted, fried and with the adrenal glands burned out. The chimney adds to the difficulty as it "sucks up" benefical ch'i.

**Solutions:** Covering the fireplace with a curtain or screen is very important – not clear glass but opaque. It is also suggested that three plants in ceramic or terra cotta pots are positioned in front and to the sides of the fireplace to control the over stimulating aspect of the fire. Earthy colors or calming images may also assist in keeping the fire under control. The excessive Fire Element also has a way of stimulating people sitting close to a fireplace to have "heated" discussions.

Avoid putting pictures of your family and loved ones on or above the mantle place so as not to "burn" them up. Remember the subconscious-primitive mind interprets reality differently than the so-called rational-pragmatic mind. Pictures depicting water or other "cooling" images would help "cool" down the "fire."

- **Stairway:** A stairway in the center of the house, like a chimney flue, draws the energy up while also being the scene of much traffic as individuals run up and down the stairs. This is more stressful to the heart and blood pressure than to the adrenals but ultimately it too is quite exhausting.

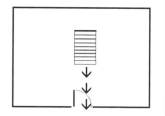

**Solutions:** A stairway in the center of a house needs to be anchored. This may be accomplished with potted plants at the base of the stairs and the kind and quality of pictures that may be hung on the walls along the stairway. A 40mm lead-glass crystal sphere can be hung from the ceiling or the chandelier if there is one. The crystal sphere will diffuse the excessive ch'i being funneled upwards.

- **Bathroom:** A bathroom in the center of the home provides too much water and too many drains. This excess of the Water Element in the center will result in kidney and urinary tract problems, or in some it may just represent water retention.

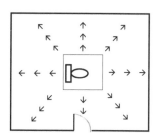

**Solutions:** The excess Water Element of the bathroom can be controlled with the proper selection of colors for paint, towels and accessories. Yellow, beige or other earth tones are colors that will absorb water. It is also helpful to keep the bathroom clean and clear of all clutter. Hanging a 30mm or 40mm lead-glass crystal sphere would also be helpful.

### 54. Very high ceilings, cathedral or vaulted ceilings.

The challenge is to achieve a feeling of intimacy and connectedness which very high ceilings and heavily sloped-ceilings tend to destroy. Evaluating a high ceiling can only be done with personal feelings. Some people like the feeling of a baronial mansion with a baronial fireplace in a baronial bedroom, and so forth. Large spaces give a feeling of grandeur and wealth. But more often a high ceilings and huge rooms result in feeling engulfed by the enor-

"The central area of the house is the 'central palace.' The importance in geomancy of the central palace is known in all cultures. An action at the center of a home may affect all areas, influencing the health and energies of the residents."
~~ Steven Post, *The Modern Book of Feng Shui*

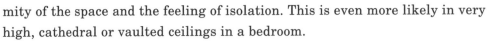

mity of the space and the feeling of isolation. This is even more likely in very high, cathedral or vaulted ceilings in a bedroom.

Cathedral ceilings have the additional problem of being sloped and thereby forcing a concentration of ch'i to flow downward upon whomever may be sitting or sleeping on that side of the room. High ceilings at the entrance way allows incoming ch'i to thin out and disperse rapidly and may indicate that along with the lack of intimacy there is also a lack of focus and difficulty keeping things under control.

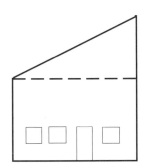

**Solutions:** The size of the room and the height of the ceiling may make bringing this situation into balance too difficult. First consider existing factors like size and positioning of doorways, windows, the view out of the windows and structural components such as beams, fireplaces and so forth. Crown molding, wall-paper border trim, or a change in color nine to ten-feet from the floor can symbolize the separation between the "heavenly" and "earthly" realms creating intimacy below and loftiness above. Also consider how you are going to decorate with furniture, wall art, mirrors, window treatments and hanging plants. Remember, the goal is to achieve intimacy and connectedness.

### 55. Exposed beams and roof supports.

Exposed beams and roof supports in effect obstruct the movement of ch'i across the ceiling and compress the ch'i forcing it downward. Those sitting under beams or roof supports therefore subconsciously experience the sensation that they are holding up the beam that is holding up the roof. This will result in feelings of a great deal of stress. Though the rational mind is quite certain the beam is firmly bolted in place, the subconscious-primitive mind continually worries, "What if it falls?"

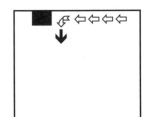

Beside the muscular stress, inflammation of soft tissue is also likely depending on an individual's constitutional type. In general, people will avoid sitting under a beam and so a beam directly over a couch or armchair will often remain unused.

**Solutions:** In evaluating the impact of an overhead beam take into consideration how high above the head it is, whether it is rounded or notched, and whether it is, or can be, painted the same color as the ceiling in order to diminish its intensity. Skillfully applied *faux* finishes can create the illusion that there is no beam. In many cases hanging fabric over exposed beams can be quite sufficient in making them disappear. Flutes are also suggested as they will appear to be lifting them upward. Some beams can be decorated with symbols, painted designs or with a series of objects such as masks to help them blend in and/or allow the ch'i to symbolically "flow through" them. But the best beams of all are no beams at all.

### 56. Sudden changes in the height of the ceiling or low archways between rooms.

Architects can get real creative producing homes with angular rooms or ceilings with changes in the height of the ceiling and many sudden drops in low passage ways or low archways between rooms. Sudden changes in ceiling heights forces the inhabitants to "expand" and "contract" as they walk from room-to-room. The design might look good on paper but is disastrous for those trying to live in spaces like this.

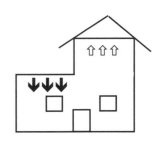

**Solutions:** Some homes I have been in are really not fit for human occupation. However, many of them can be balanced by the judicial use of wall-hangings and upward lighting using soft-yin elements to balance the hard-yang and the yang elements to balance the yin. Gentle moving mobiles can be hung in any corner where the ch'i might stagnate.

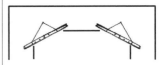

Try filling in large wall spaces with Oriental carpets, Indian blankets, or other large decorative wall hangings or sculpture. Over low narrow passage ways you can hang decorative fans that give the illusion of an archway. Or use bamboo flutes on archways or beams to reduce the straight line and change the angles.

There are so many varieties of drop-ceilings from thin strips directly over the head of the bed and around the periphery of a room, low archways dividing one room from another to someone's idea of an added-on room. Like any art project the eye has to travel smoothly from shape-to-shape aided by color, texture, shape and imagery.

### 57. Sloped-ceilings over sitting areas.

Sloped-ceilings over sitting areas force the ch'i moving along the ceiling to rapidly descend causing discomfort to those who continually sit under them. Even seeing a section of the ceiling slope elsewhere in the house can have a disorienting effect which the subconscious mind interprets as life-out-of-balance. But worst of all is the slope coming down behind where you sleep or sit at a desk putting pressure and tension on the neck and shoulders.

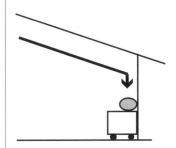

**Solutions:** It is usually adequate to hang a bamboo flute with the mouth piece down and the other end pointing up at a 45° angle to reverse the negative influences of a sloped-ceiling. Larger bamboo flutes are stronger than flutes made from reeds. Bamboo flutes are often recommended as bamboo represent strength as they grow upward notch-by-notch. They are also resilient and get extra power as a musical instrument. However, not everyone can aesthetically decide to put bamboo over their Chippendale furniture, so other solutions have to be found that serve the same function. Perhaps a sculpture or wall-hanging with an upward momentum. Good luck in coming up with an alternative solution.

### 58. Very low ceilings.

Rooms with low ceilings or rooms that are too small in relationship to the activity of the room generate feelings of constraint and claustrophobia. A nine-foot ceiling is most comfortable while an eight-foot or even seven-foot ceiling feels most contractive. This is especially true for tall or large people or in rooms filled with oversized furniture. How you evaluate this situation may depend on what the room is being used for. If the room is being used for quiet activities, it may be quite comfortable, womb-like and intimate. If the room is designated for a busy activity, like cooking or working, such a room may make some individuals feel like they have no elbow-room and are trapped.

**Solutions:** Decorating with bright light, mirrors and low furniture may provide a feeling of expansiveness in an otherwise contractive situation. If the whole house has ceilings that feel too low, I would probably not consider renting or buying unless I was of shorter stature and felt I could adequately decorate to create the illusion of more spaciousness.

If you remove a low flat ceiling exposing a peaked roof along with the rafters, be sure to cover the rafters with a new ceiling (page 68, #55 - Exposed beams and roof supports). Though giving height to the ceiling the new ceiling will be sloped and this will make it uncomfortable to sit or sleep unless you decorate with bamboo flutes or other upward pointing wall-hangings to counter the down-pushing ch'i (page 69, #57 - Sloped-ceilings over sitting areas).

### 59. Pillars and free-standing structural supports.

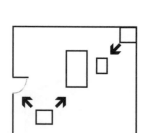

Pillars and free-standing structural supports that are rounded are better than square which shoot "hidden arrows" in four or more directions. Pillars, whether designed as columns or merely a 4 x 4 support, divide the view and make for fracturing of personalities. Exposed corner structural supports are also aggressive and send "arrows" across a room.

**Solutions:** As with beams, it is best to remove all pillars if possible. If they are structurally important, your next challenge is to decorate them by blending them into the background in order to diminish their impact. With pillars or other structural supports this can be done by training vining plants to grow around them, by wrapping them with ribbons or silk vines, or even painting flowering vines or other playful images upon them.

### 60. Sunken living rooms.

Sunken living rooms are disorienting to the psyche as the hallways and stairways of a home are like rivers and streams along which ch'i flows. When the ch'i comes to a sunken living room, it puddles and has no where to go and no way to get out. It stagnates. Split levels result in split opinions and split

families with many arguments as the in-coming ch'i gets confused. If the energy of the home is confused, the people of the home will probably be confused too. A home with many levels can also indicate that life has many ups and downs financially and emotionally.

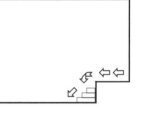

**Solutions:** Potted plants on either side of stairs leading down to the sunken living room will add some life and help deter less observing individuals from stumbling down. As Denny Fairchild suggests in *Healing Homes: Then & Now*, "do what theatres do to avoid litigation. Outline every down stair with tiny Christmas tree lights, illuminating from the ground up. This prevents spilled drinks, hip fractures and opens up the opportunity for a harmonious household." A throw carpet at the bottom may also provide a "landing zone" and a place to reorientate before moving on to the new level. Perhaps a mobile could be hung in the most stagnant corner to keep the ch'i moving. Or a 30mm or 40mm lead-glass crystal sphere in the center of the room to "lift" the ch'i up.

If the sunken room also has large windows or sliding glass doors, the house will "leak" prosperity like a sieve. Make sure the windows are adequately curtained and decorated to catch the life-giving ch'i before it flows out. In short, it is best to avoid a house with a sunken living room or lots of awkward levels.

### 61. Irregularly shaped rooms (not square or rectangular) or with slanted walls.

It is best when ch'i flows smoothly and unobstructed. Irregular-shaped rooms with many angles usually mean turbulent areas as ch'i gets stuck in corners "trying to decide which way to go." As someone once pointed out, "the areas of life most out of tune are reflected in the rooms most out of shape."

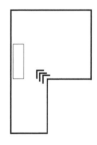

In rooms with many angles, "hidden arrows" shoot out accordingly. Especially important is to notice if any angles are angling at you in your bed, dining room table, home office, or other frequently used location. I have often noticed that the area of the room on the "other side" of the angle is rarely if ever used as the subconscious avoids passing between two wall angles.

In rooms with one wall slanted inward the subconscious need for stability is also upset and may reflect a distorted sense of reality. Or, if the room is small, a feeling of claustrophobia may result. If it is a frequently used room such as a bedroom, living room or office, a room with a slanted wall will result in anxiety, uncertainty, and poor decision making.

**Solutions:** In a room with many angles, the three primary ways to nullify "hidden arrows" are to remove it, block it or deflect it. In this situation the most obvious method is to block the offending edge either with tall potted plants, by tacking up edge-molding, or even by thumb tacking a decorative

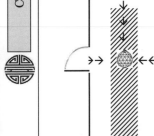

scarf over the protruding edge. Some irregularly shaped rooms are very difficult to harmonize and require great creativity in how you round that angle out or position furniture so as not to end up in a doorway or beneath a beam.

In a room with a slanted wall the best solution to try is positioning a mirror on the slanted-wall to reflect the opposite wall to give the impression that the slanted-wall is also properly squared off at the corners. A large potted plant in the corner forming an obtuse angle may also satisfactorily square off the room. If the room is a frequently used room, "squaring" the room is more important than a room that is rarely used.

### 62. Long narrow hallways.

Ch'i moves fast in the home when it moves in a long straight line as in long hallways or from one area of the house to another without a doorway or wall to slow it down. This results in people of the house frequently racing through this area and comes to symbolize "racing through life" from one location to another or from one project to another. Always something to do and always something to do fast. Always racing. Eventually always exhausted. Eventually finding it difficult to keep up. As a long narrow hallway has visual similarity to the intestines, a long hall can represent intestinal problems.

**Solutions:** If there are long hallways, you need to evaluate how they are to be handled, and whether the fast-moving energy they represent is also inherent in other features of the home under consideration. The longer and darker the long narrow hallway is, the more foreboding and anxiety producing it is. So use bright colors, good lighting, mirrors or picture art with positive images to slow the ch'i down.

To slow down in life it is essential to slow down the ch'i flow through the house in those places that it "races." This can be done in many ways. One is to lay down a section of carpet, interestingly enough referred to as a "runner." But it is important to choose a runner that has a design on it. A design that meanders allows the eye to "meander" even if only seen by the peripheral vision. To further assist in this meandering effect, pictures and other hanging objects can be hung on the walls to help the eye zig-zag along.

Things can also be hung from the ceiling at appropriate intervals such as lead-glass crystal spheres, wind chimes, mobiles, or whatever fits your aesthetic and in accordance with the actual length of hallway or areas of the house. Lead-glass crystal spheres are especially effective where there are doorways to rooms that are accessed along the long hallway in question. Do not put a mirror at the end of a long hallway as that will make it longer. Remember to avoid creating obstructions or hanging large bulky picture frames that someone might bump into.

### 63. A room situated at the end of a long narrow hallway.

It is especially unfortunate to have a bedroom, office or any frequently used room located at the end of a long hallway as the "killing ch'i" continuously "bombards" those within. As with a parking area facing a bedroom or entrance way (page 50, #31) or a house on a T-section roadway (page 50, #32), avoid "hidden arrows" produced by fast moving ch'i that is moving in your direction.

A bathroom at the end of a long hallway or directly in line with the front door funnels the good ch'i right down the toilet. An office at the end of a long hall generates constant anxiety – like living or sitting on a railroad track. Very distracting and very nerve wracking.

**Solutions:** As with any long narrow hallways, the first challenge is to slow the ch'i flow down. This can be accomplished with a runner carpet, one long one or two short ones. Preferably a carpet with a "meandering" design. If the hall is wide enough for pictures or wall-hangings, this too is suggested. At least one 30mm lead-glass crystal sphere hanging from the ceiling midway down the hall or outside the door to any room or rooms that may open into the long narrow hall will serve to diffuse the fast moving ch'i.

Actually remedying the room at the end of the narrow hall is more problematic. Some practitioners might suggest a mirror to "bounce" the ch'i away from either the bathroom, bedroom or office that may be the recipient of the "killing" ch'i. If a mirror is used, it should be large enough to be able to see your head and shoulders in while walking toward it, yet small enough not to create the reflected illusion that the hall is longer than it already is. I prefer a framed-picture depicting a scene that gives a sense of depth. A framed-picture of a landscape or distant view will absorb the fast flowing ch'i while the glass covering the picture will bounce the ch'i back as a mirror would but without the reflection that doubles the image of the hallway.

Whether a mirror or a picture, it should be affixed to the door securely. Not just hung loosely so that it will rattle and bang every time the door is opened or closed. Most home improvement stores sell tacky, putty-like stuff that can be pressed onto the back of the lower corners of the mirror or picture to keep it from moving. If a framed-picture is chosen, non-breakable plexiglas can be used instead of the more fragile glass that picture frames usually come with. Plexiglas instead of a thin piece of glass should alleviate the "what if the glass breaks" uncertainty.

### 64. No back door or back window, or rooms with no windows at all.

No back door or back window is another case of the ch'i having no where to go. The ch'i that comes in the front door, ideally circulates through each of the rooms of the house and then goes out again. If there are no back windows or doors, the ch'i is trapped and stagnates. This problem of stagnant ch'i is more severe in rooms that are frequently used.

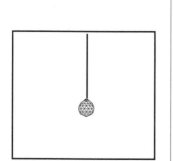

**Solutions:** It is important to create a symbolic back door or window using one's imagination and perhaps framed pictures on the wall that provide the impression of looking out into the distance. It is also necessary from time to time to stir up the ch'i of such rooms using mobiles, aromatherapy diffusers, wind chimes, Tibetan bells or whatever else will change the vibration and recharge it.

### 65. Large Windows, floor-length windows, or sliding glass doors.

Large windows, floor-length windows, or sliding glass doors with wonderful views are inspirational and are especially dazzling to the visitor. However, for those living in such dwellings picture windows, many large windows on a wall, floor length windows, or sliding glass doors can have the result of being too overwhelming as they allow excessive amounts of bright light to enter the room and good energy to easily leave due to lack of containment.

Large windows have the effect of being too distracting, undermining focus and concentration. If the view is to the west, it can also strain the eyes as late in the day the western glare is the most intense. As one authority, Denny Fairchild, stated, large uncovered windows make a person "nervous, hyperactive and a definite candidate for Prozac."

**Solutions:** In these situations it is most important to be able to "calm down" the nervous system by quieting down the excessive ch'i. This can be accomplished with window treatments that soften the framing of the window as it contrasts the subdued interior with the bright exterior. Window curtains should also be able to be closed so that when the brightness of outside is too intense that the curtains can be closed.

In addition to the window curtains which impart a softer and more intimate feeling to the room, other window coverings can be installed to get closure or to diffuse the in-coming light such as venetian blinds, roll up bamboo, or rice paper shades. Vertical blinds and mini-blinds are to be avoided as they emanate "hidden arrows" by slicing through the room like a "tomato cutter." If vertical, horizontal or mini-blinds are installed they should be kept either totally closed or completely pulled open in order to avoid their "slicing" effect (compare page 132, #154 - Remove louvered windows and vertical blinds).

For floor-length windows and sliding glass doors potted plants can be positioned outside or inside or a low bench or bookshelf can be used to provide a sense of barrier, especially if the windows are high off the ground and looking down creates a vertigo.

To further diffuse the in-coming brightness without having to close the curtains or window shades, you can hang lead-glass crystal spheres and other window decorations like dried flowers pressed between two pieces of glass, stained-glass window hanging, or hand-blown glass ornaments. Get creative but don't over-decorate. Lots of smaller window panes, especially wooden window panes, reduces the negative impact of large windows.

### 66. View of tree trunk, lamp post or utility pole through a window.

A view of a tree trunk, lamp post or utility pole through a window affects the eyes. Just as the doors represent "mouths," the walls the "skin," and so forth, the windows of the house symbolize the "eyes." The eyes are directly connected to the liver and in time the liver function will also be undermined by a tree trunk, lamp post or utility pole blocking the view through a window.

**Solutions:** Of course distance from the offending tree trunk, lamp post or utility pole is the first determining factor in determining severity of this situation. It is not so much as how far in inches, feet or yards but rather how close does it feel in relationship to the size of the window and the view of the tree trunk, lamp post or utility pole. Consider whether you can decorate the section of the tree that is in view in order to soften it and make it appear more friendly and not so bold.

Decorations can include bird feeders, bird houses, wind chimes, a faceted lead-glass crystal prism in the window, or even tying colorful fabric strips around the tree trunk, lamp post or utility pole (compare page 75, #66 - Tree trunk, lamp post, telephone or utility pole directly opposite the front door of the house). A window in a frequently used room will be more detrimental than a window in a less frequently used room.

### 67. All doors, no windows.

A home built without windows and all doors is an arrangement that is often found in Spanish hacienda-style houses where double doors provide the openness to a courtyard or patio. The problem with this arrangement is that the windows represent the "voice of the children" while the doors represent the "voice of the parents." They should be in a proper proportion which feng shui lore indicates to be three windows to each door.

Consequently, in a home with no windows the children have no voice and the parents dominate. Often this results in the children having serious physical or psychological problems in their attempt to be "heard."

**Solutions:** The best solution of course is to move. If moving is not an option or until moving is possible, you can hang pictures on the walls that appear to be window-like. Choose pictures featuring landscapes and distant views, perhaps with frames that also assist in the illusion that these are the windows. The pictures need to be hung with great intention that they represent windows or else it is merely a weak band-aid in effectiveness.

### 68. Skylights anywhere in the home.

In a bedroom a skylight is like having an observing "eye in the sky" watching every action. Likewise, over a stove or desk, the excessive ch'i is a weakening influence. A skylight elsewhere in the home may be appropriately

placed to bring light into an otherwise dark area. In an area of the home that does not receive direct light a skylight can be thought of as invigorating. While in an already bright part of the home, a skylight can be overwhelming as excessive ch'i bears down upon the inhabitants and ch'i either thins out or rushes out of the house.

Wherever a skylight is going to be located, installing a skylight needs to be treated with great care similar to doing surgery on the human body. Installing a skylight into the roof of a home can have dire consequences if not done with the proper respect and consideration. It is the usual lack of respect and consideration that often coincides with one of the members of the household needing an actual surgery. This phenomenon can only be attributed to the extent that people living in a home actually do become identified with their homes and that the home become an extension of their own bodies: the doors like mouths, windows eyes, walls skin and so forth.

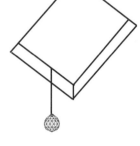

**Solutions:** To avoid this negative consequence approach the "surgery" of the home with great respect by doing prayers, perhaps performing a ritual that is in harmony with your religious or spiritual beliefs. To keep it simple merely light a candle in the area of the home to be "operated" upon. Perhaps burn some incense, ring bells, and say a prayer that no one in the home will be effected by the cutting of the roof for installing the skylight. Give thanks and praise and see the project proceeding smoothly from beginning to end.

Once the skylight is installed, or if you rented or purchased a home with skylights already in place, it is consider good feng shui to hang a multi-faceted, leaded-glass crystal prism from a nine-inch red ribbon. The crystal prism will diffuse the excessive day light ch'i in addition to energizing the area of the home it is hanging in.

### 69. Three doorways in a row – "a pierced heart."

Three doorways in a row is called the "pierced heart" by some practitioners. Though the heart may not be directly effected, certainly the maladies that develop in such houses confirm that there is much sadness and that the heart is at least symbolically "pierced." It is especially detrimental to work, stand or sit for many hours in such a situation. Whether it is your desk, stove or dining room table, get out of the "line of fire." A desk may be easy to relocate, a dining room table between two doors will rarely if ever be used, and moving a stove is usually too costly and unlikely.

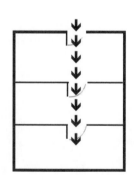

Even two doorways in a row will tend to propel us and the ch'i rapidly ahead especially if there is a door opposite the front door itself. Homes with two or more doorways in a row tend to be draftier as the ch'i flows quickly from one end of the home to another. This may be another reason three doorways is considered an indicator of poor health which would be especially severe in colder climates.

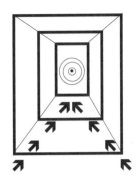

**Solutions:** Hanging curtains on doorways or keeping them closed may be adequate depending on how close they are to each other and their frequency of usage. A traditional approach is to hang bamboo flutes behind each door way to draw the ch'i forward while slowing it down. Evaluate this situation very carefully. In most cases, houses with three doorways in a row are probably houses that should be remodeled to remove one of the doorways. If the house cannot be remodeled, choose a different house to live in.

### 70. Three or more doors very close together in a row.

When confronted by a row of doors, the human response is to make a decision. Making choices are not easy if each door appears exactly alike. If the doors are positioned next to each other on the same wall, the indecisiveness is increased. As in the story, *The Lady & the Tiger*, "which door is danger and which success" becomes the nagging question confronting the subconscious each time you walk towards a wall with two or more doors.

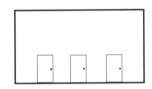

**Solutions:** The situation is easily rectified by hanging something symbolic on each door giving each one a unique character or painting each doorway a different color.

### 71. Three or more doors close together leading into different directions.

In this situation the problem is not so much an indecisiveness of choice, which door to choose, as it an anticipation of someone, or something, suddenly emerging from one of the other rooms and crashing into you. This is often an arrangement of a bathroom between two bedrooms.

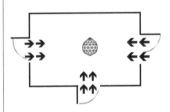

**Solutions:** Hanging a faceted lead-glass crystal sphere from the ceiling on a nine- inch red ribbon might be sufficient. The lead-glass crystal sphere will serve as kind of a "traffic cop" to "sort out" the ch'i flow from each doorway. Placing an area rug in front of the doors will also help slow the conflicting ch'i down by giving it a "place to rest."

### 72. Double doors at the front entrance or entrance into any room.

As with more than one doorway in a small area, double doors into a house or individual room, encourages a feeling of uncertainty and therefore confusion. Which door is opened and which is locked? Which is used and which is not?

Another problem caused by double doors is that ch'i rapidly rushes in when the doors are open or are left open. This can be especially detrimental to health and stability if the double doors open into a bedroom or home office and the bed or the desk is in direct line with the doorway. In these situations disorders of the nervous system or exhausted adrenals can develop as an individual in bed or sitting at the desk remains hyper alert in anticipation of someone, or something, unexpectedly barging in.

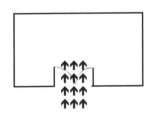

**Solutions:** One obvious suggestion is to keep one door permanently locked. If it is the front door of the house, perhaps a door knocker or some other accessory associated with the front door can be hung on the side that is to be used so the ch'i knows which door to enter through. If the double doors lead into a home office or bedroom, keep one door locked and hang something on the door to signify which side is being used.

The aspect of the problem which is harder to remedy is the feeling of uncertainty that someone or something can suddenly barge in without warning and without the opportunity to gather one's wits let alone a means of protection. To help mitigate this fear and lingering anxiety a small wind chime can be hung inside the door to draw negative energy upward or two Fu dogs (dragon headed dogs) can be place outside on either side of the entrance way as guardians. Two plants, two lions or any imposing duplicates can be used to signal protection for those within. A small area rug will also assis in slowing the fast incoming ch'i down. But all-in-all a double door into a room is difficult to bring into balance especially if the doors are further destabilized by being hung on an angle (page 78, #74 – Doors hung at an angle – "evil door.").

### 73. Misaligned doorways – "a bad bite."

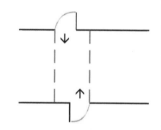

In this situation the doorways of two rooms situated off a hallway or not very wide corridor are opposite each other but are off-set or more appropriately described as "misaligned." The ch'i does not flow smoothly into either room. Misaligned doorways create an imbalance in the mind's constant attempt to perceive the world in balance and symmetry. One eye sees distance while the other eye is forced to focus at something nearby. If this is a frequent situation, it will result in left brain-right brain imbalance, emotional uncertainty, and will have an effect on physical and emotional equilibrium (page 92, #100 – Split wall as you enter).

**Solutions:** The remedy for this situation is to bring the two doorways into balance by hanging framed-pictures with glass over the picture to widen the door outline and to provide a sense of depth so both eyes can focus simultaneously. How much space is on either side and the distance between the misaligned doors will determine whether a reflective surface is needed, or if a simple wall-hanging will create the illusion that each door is wider and properly aligned.

### 74. Doorways hung at an angle – "evil door."

Doorways at an angle can be very detrimental if they open into a bedroom. Even worse is a double door opening into a master bedroom. An angled-doorway opening into a study, den, less frequently used room, or an activity room is not so problematic. Intimacy and restful security are not of impor-

tance as they would be in a bedroom.

A doorway set at an angle that opens into a bedroom often opens in direct alignment with the bed itself making this a variation of the room at the end of a long narrow hallway (page 73, #63) or the Coffin Position discussed below (page 100, #112). Too much ch'i rushes in too fast and all at once. The unexpected can happen with no time to regain composure or to protect oneself. Preparedness for a sudden emergency needs to be maintained. Angled-doorways indicate stressful high anxiety.

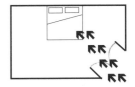

**Solutions:** If you are stuck with a home with an angled bedroom door, close it at night. Locking it might provide a greater sense of security while sleeping. To balance the awkwardness of an angled door it is suggested to hang a 40mm lead-glass crystal sphere both on the inside and outside of the doorway. The right choice of uplifting decorative wall-hangings will also assist in making the transition in and out of an angled bedroom door psychologically easier as well.

## 75. Doors that open to the smallest part of a room – "contrary doors."

A door, especially the front door, should open so you can see the majority of the room. "Contrary doors" limit ch'i flow into a house or into a room. Not being able to see the larger portion of a room generates feelings of insecurity as the person entering does not know what to expect. If this is a frequently used door, the inhabitants are likely to feel uptight all the time with constant tension in the neck and shoulders. Frequent head aches are also probable.

**Solutions:** The best solution for a "contrary door" is to rehinge the door so that it opens to reveal the larger portion of a room. If this is not possible, you can try hanging a mirror on the wall enabling anyone entering to be able to see a reflection of the larger portion of the room so they can feel more relaxed. This is similar to using a mirror or other reflective surfaces on your desk, wall opposite your bed or any other situation where you can not see the door. Note: If you use a mirror in this situation, be sure it is hung for the tallest person living or working where there is a "contrary door."

## 76. Less important doorways larger than doorways of more important rooms.

Whenever one door is larger than another, the larger door is perceived as intimidating to those coming out of the smaller door. This is acceptable if the smaller door is a closet, utility room, or even bathroom. It is not acceptable when the smaller door is a living room, bedroom or home office and the larger door is a closet, utility room, or bathroom (page 59, #45 – "tiger's mouth"). Less important rooms with large doorways perpetuate a feeling of being diminished and eventually undermine self-esteem and sense of personal accomplishment.

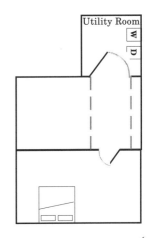

Utility Room

W

D

**Solutions:** As with misaligned doors (page 78, #73) or a split wall at the front door (page 92, #100), a mirror or other reflective surface can be mounted on the side of the smaller door to give the impression that it is larger and to give a sense of depth to enable both eyes to see deep and to maintain left brain-right brain balance which, when disturbed, undermines agility and accessibility to intuitive or rational decision making.

### 77. An "empty doorway".

If there is a doorway that once had a door hanging in it but now is without that door though the door frame still has cut outs for the hinges and lock then it is an "empty door." Projects that are incomplete, household features that are broken or not working well, all affect the subconscious of the inhabitants which will translate into incompletions and feeling that whatever is being done is not quite complete.

**Solutions:** Either rehang the door or, if the door was removed for practical purposes such as providing easy passage through a corridor or not having an open door take up wall space, then redo the door frame to remove the hinge and lock cut outs and make the doorway into an official archway.

### 78. Doors that clash – "arguing door knobs."

If two doors when opened at the same time are positioned so close together that the door knobs will hit each other, this is called "arguing" door knobs. Consequently, this area of the house experiences constant turmoil due to the aggressiveness of the two doors banging, or potentially banging, into each other. When ch'i flow "clashes" anywhere in the home and for any reason, the result is members of the household will be constantly arguing.

**Solution:** The best solution would be to rehinged the two doors so they will open away from each other. If this is not practical, either because of financial reasons or because either of the rehinged doors will be creating other difficulties, then a transcendental solution can be tried: tie a red ribbon from one door knob to the other visually connecting them leaving the ends long enough to tie into bows. Once the two door knobs are connected, cut the ribbon in half and tie the ends into a bow. Now the two door knobs have symbolically become friends. A small wind chime representing harmony can also be hung from the ceiling midway above and between the two doors to bring harmony to the "arguing" door knobs.

### 79. Dutch doors – top half can open separately from bottom half.

Dutch doors, often associated with a country home ambience, allows one to feel "secure" by closing the bottom half while letting fresh air to flow in by leaving the top half opened. From a feng shui perspective doors need to

appear solid so "dutch doors" are like two doors that are "incomplete" – each half being half a door.

**Solution:** Both halves should be bolted together and only used as a whole door. Often curtains are hung on only the upper half and instead curtains should be hung to cover both the top and bottom half giving the appearance of one solid door.

### 80. Any door opens outward instead of inward.

A door that opens outward "blocks" the ch'i flow from coming into the home. It feels awkward and aggressive having to open a door against the prevalent flow of ch'i. Ch'i flows more smoothly when a door opens inward. An inward opening door will feel more accommodating and inviting. This is especially important for the front door of residence or a place of business which needs the ch'i to flow in easily and unobstructed.

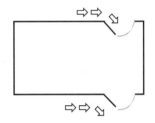

**Solutions:** If the door of a home or business does open outward obstructing the flow of easy ch'i flow, the door should be rehung to open inward. If it is not feasible to rehang the door to open inward perhaps due to fire code, hanging a wind chime, 40mm lead-glass crystal sphere, and other decorations on either side of the doorway may ease the transition for the person entering to take their subconscious off of the awkwardness of having to open a door outwards in order to go inward. If store front has an outward opening door, it may be possible during business hours and when the weather is warm to leave the door fully open so customers can easily enter.

### 81. Spiral staircase or staircases that are steep or unsteady.

Spiral staircases are the worst as they "corkscrew" through the home as if someone is drilling into one's body, or into the "heart." In addition to the psychological impact, they are clumsy and feel dangerous to walk up or down. Kids like to play on them and can easily get hurt especially if they are metal steps with open risers.

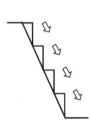

**Solutions:** It is best to remove these stairs and replace with a staircase that is more secure and easier to use. If this is not possible, consider hanging wind chimes and lead-glass crystals above the staircase to protect you from their negative consequences. Placing several potted plants beneath the stair will also help to harmonize this negative feature especially if they have open risers and "floating stairs" which are most common in spiral staircases.

If these are the only stairs connecting two levels of the home, evaluate carefully if they can be removed, or if the countermeasures suggested can be adequately applied. It is more than likely that it is best not to buy or rent a house with a spiral staircase.

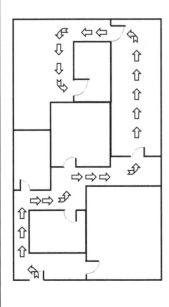

**82. City streets to the house, hallways in an apartment complex, or the floor plan of the house like a maze.**

It is nice to be able to go straight to where you are headed. Being unimpeded in one's journey is conducive to maintaining a relaxed disposition. Hallways and stairways are conduits for ch'i to flow along. The ch'i should flow easily and unimpeded to your front door. Hallways in apartment complexes or winding street-like mazes make the ch'i flow confused with their twists and turns. Even though, you, as a resident, may get familiar with the tortuous route, there is part of the subconscious that is forever struggling as it tries to remember which twists and which turn to take next. The mouse eventually gets the cheese through learned behavior as the researcher cheers it on. But the tension level remains high until the goal is achieved.

**Solutions:** Avoid housing situations such as these. If your circumstance does not allow for change, attempt to clearly mark your path with visual aids that are easy to recognize and easy to describe to a stranger who may one day have to find their way to your house with a winning check for a million dollars.

*Taiji*
*The balance of opposites relative to each other,*
*each within each other, encircled by unity.*

# Attracting Opportunities

## Evaluating the Entrance

Does your front door need a fresh coat of paint? Or address numbers that shine? Is the front lawn green or ghastly? Like a business card, your front entrance connects the outside world with your own.

~~ Denny Fairchild, *Healing Homes*: Feng Shui Here & Now

The front door that was built as the front door of the home is considered to be the "mouth of ch'i" and it is usually further designated by being the entrance way that has the numbers of the home's street address near or on it as well as the door bell or door knocker. Very often the mailbox is also situated near it. It is most important that this entrance be well-lit and free of obstruction both as you look out from it and as you enter through it.

Certainly the door itself should be of good appearance. A broken door should be fixed. A fresh coat of paint or application of a wood preservative each year is recommended. Other factors should also be considered: is the front door easy to find, well-lit at night, are the pathway(s) to your door clear and unobstructed, is there a view from the door as you look out, is the space in front of your door and on the inside wide enough, and so forth.

The condition of the front door is more than just its appearance. As the "mouth" of the house, it is where the home's "nourishment" comes in. Good ch'i coming in equates to good health and opportunities. With this in mind keep the front door and entranceway looking good and keep it uncluttered so it can open wide. Notice if there are any attacking structures or forms, man made or natural in origin, that might be "shooting" at you as you stand in the entry. If you can not remove them, do your best to block or deflect them to ensure only good ch'i comes in your door (compare page 57, Neighbors: Harmony in the Community).

It might be beneficial to attempt to walk up to your front door as if you are a stranger bringing those living in the house some really good news. As you approach the house from the street, be aware of how easy or difficult this task might be. Perhaps walk up with a good friend and get their feedback as well. Does your home feel abundant, expansive and secure? Consider all the adjustments that could be made to improve your "path in life" and your ability to attract opportunities.

This exercise is especially valuable if you usually enter the house from the garage or a side or back door and if you rarely use the front door on a regular

> "As a rule, the best entrances give an open, spacious, even grand feeling."
> ~~ Sarah Rossbach, *Interior Design with Feng Shui*

> "The threshold, or front door, of your home is very important, as it represents your relationship with society."
> ~~ Terah Kathryn Collins, *The Western Guide to Feng Shui*

> "When Chi is not accessible, you must invite it into your space and encourage it to stay. Chi is attracted by light, living things, and objects that catch the eye, like a beautiful painting. It is attracted to bold colors, pleasant sounds, running water, plants, and flowers. Whatever pleasantly attracts your attention, attracts Chi."
> ~~ Angel Thompson, *The Feng Shui Anthology: Contemporary Earth Design,* edited by Jami Lin

basis. Areas of the house or apartment that are rarely used tend to be the most neglected and yet all areas are internalized and are responded to on the subconscious level. Taking a look at an area that is being neglected can be very revealing to your own process of self development. You may find the entrance way to your home is an excellent place to examine some deeply embedded core issues.

### Path of Daily Ch'i.

If a different door other than the front door is used everyday to enter and leave the home such as a garage door, side or back door, this door is called the "Path of Daily Ch'i." This pathway in and out of the home should also be unobstructed, pleasant to pass through, and free of clutter and obstructions making it easy to use. However, do use the front door from time to time to keep it energized.

### 83. A home with a view from the front entrance way.

A view from the front door unobstructed by pillars, trees, mountains or whatever is of major importance to anyone who is an innovator, an entrepreneur, or living a creative lifestyle. If the front door opens to a view, you will have inspiration and vision.

It is said that if from your front door you can only see the street, your opportunities will come only from your small community. If you can look out over a larger area, opportunities will come from outside your community. If you can see a lake or ocean, your opportunities can come from all over and even from across the seas. Of course if you see a cemetery, police station, casino or other low vibration establishments, these will define your home in a more negative way. If you aspire to be a creative artist, an innovative entrepreneur, a freelancer, or someone who lives and works independently, than an expansive view is essential to your success and recognition.

**Solutions:** Understandably this may be difficult to find in large urban centers with street after street of high rise apartment buildings. In these situations it may be sufficient to hang pictures and paintings that symbolically provides a view on either side of the front door as you exit.

If you step out your front door and are visually confronted by a mountain or tall building, you may feel obstructed and overpowered. To compensate for this unfortunate circumstance you can hang a concave mirror to reflect and diminish the larger structure. Installing spotlights or a flag pole behind the house may also work towards restoring some semblance of balance between your smaller structure and the one before you – like a lion with a large mane.

### 84. Attracting beneficial ch'i to your doorway – an unobstructed pathway.

All doorways and pathway to the house should be unobstructed as this is how opportunities come your way. But most important of all the pathway to

the front door and the front entrance way itself is the source of the greatest nourishment. It should be easy to find and easy to get to. It should have a nice meandering path to it, be easy to stand in front of and to enter through.

**Solutions:** In the Orient, doorways are often painted red as red is the color that attracts the most energy. It is highly recommended that each year, or two, perhaps at the beginning of the year, or the beginning of spring after the severity of the winter has past, that you apply fresh paint or wood preservative to your front door to energize its opportunity-attracting ability. Prune back foliage as needed and replace outworn doormats with more attractive ones. Use potted plants, sculpture and whatever else might attract beneficial ch'i to your home.

Hanging brass wind chimes can be very beneficial as the tubes of the wind chime funnel negative ch'i up and away, and the clear, crisp sound attracts opportunity to you, as you "sound" forth to the world. The world knows where to find you. Beware, however, that the wind chime is of the appropriate size. Bigger isn't better. A wind chime that is too big or is making noise all the time due to constant winds and hanging in a windy location will chase your good fortune away.

Placement of the numbers of your street address can also be used in a positive way. If they are old and corroded, trade them in for bright and shiny ones. Neither too small and obscure nor too large and ostentatious. Pin them to the siding of your house or on your mailbox so each number is progressively higher than the last giving an upward motion as another affirmation of your success and upward progress in life. Feng shui principles can be applied to even seemingly minor details.

### 85. Clearly defined pathway to the front door.

No clear path to the front door equals few, if any, opportunities. The driveway is like a path but not to the actual entrance way. A pathway from the driveway is often found in homes built on crowded housing developments. In most situations this is adequate. But a clearly defined pathway that is separate from the driveway is best.

Driving onto a dirt lot in front of a home without clearly defined parking area or pathway to the front door. leaves too much to the imagination with the inhabitants feeling vulnerable and unprotected like a covered wagon exposed on the open prairie with hostile natives attacking from all sides. Cars pulling up to the home from all possible directions constantly "shoot arrows" at the home. Landscaping and hardscaping is essential to determine from what direction the ch'i flows to you, and whether it feels harmonious or discordant.

**Solutions:** Best of all is a pathway directly from the sidewalk or curb that brings opportunities right to you. The path should be well-lit, easy to navigate, meandering slightly and perhaps enhanced with flowering plants along its borders.

"The entranceway and everything leading up to it is a direct reflection of who you are. The entranceway acts as a transitional space that bridges your home with the environment outside."
~~ Nancy SantoPietro,
*Feng Shui: Harmony by Design*

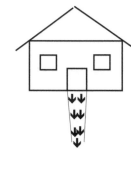

## 86. Path to the front door is narrow at one end and wide at the other.

If the path to the front door is narrower than the door, the occupants of the home will feel like they are "starving" as they also would if the pathway begins wide and narrows in width as it reaches the entrance way. If the pathway begins narrow and gets wider as it approaches the front of the house, the occupants may feel that their "path out to the world" lacks opportunity.

**Solutions:** Remedy this by making the pathway wider than the entrance way and equal in width from beginning to end. If this can not be done, an alternative is to install two light features on either side of the narrow portion of the path; to energize that area to harmonize the flow of ch'i.

## 87. Pathway in a straight line to the front door.

Another feature to avoid is a pathway or driveway to the front door that is a long, straight line. As with all things in nature, anything that is long and straight is considered unnatural compared to flowing and meandering. Streams, rivers and pathways through the forest all meander. Anything that moves straight ahead is aggressive like a fast moving river which erodes the soil and rips away the foliage growing along the embankment. To have a pathway or driveway go straight to the entrance way of the house is to "attack" the "mouth of the house" and its occupants will suffer. Also avoid front doors that are at the end of pathways between two buildings.

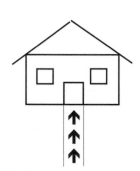

**Solutions:** As with all straight lines, the challenge is to transform them into flowing and meandering lines. If you cannot actually redesign your pathway to curve or meander to your front door then try to change the appearance of the pathway. This can be achieved with various design motifs using brick work or stamped-concrete. The placement of plants, potted or in the ground, will also help. If done right, your eyes will move back and forth as you walk ahead, causing you to slow your pace, breathe calmly and feel uplifted.

Two large potted plants on either side of the front door may also appear like sentinels guarding you from the "killing" ch'i coming your way. Pathway lighting is another way to alter the intensity of any "hidden arrows" from straight pathways. If the pathway is angular it is also a good idea to use in the ground plantings or potted plants, bird baths or other garden accessories to round out the edges to encourage the eye to meander.

## 88. Dilapidated front porch.

If the front porch is run down, in need of fresh paint, with a screen door with either squeaky hinges, falling off its hinges, overgrown with vines, cluttered with potted plants that are underwatered, underfed and oversize for their containers, cluttered by rattan furniture that is ready

to fall in heap, etc. etc. etc., the whole house must be a fixer-upper. Consider if you are up for the task.

**Solution:** Like everything else about your entrance way: a clear, unobstructed path, a nice looking solid door, easy to read house numbers and so forth, The porch area should never look shabby or unkempt. Keep it clean and freshen it up with new paint when needed. If there are plants on your porch in front of your entrance way keep them well watered, lush looking and free of brown leaves or dead flowers. Avoid pointy-leaf plants like most dracenas and all prickly cactus plants which "shoot arrows" in all directions, and remove spider plants which symbolize "multiplying" problems as the new sprouts dangle looking for a place to establish themselves and never do. Maintain the landscaping along the pathway and around the entrance and great good fortune will continue to enter your life.

## 89. Pillars across the front porch that give the appearance of a prison.

Public structures like government buildings are made more imposing by the careful positioning of columns and pillars. Even stately southern mansions take on a regal air. Caution however needs to be maintained when designing a smaller home with pillars and columns as they may result in the home being suffocated and made foreboding.

Though a pillar, porch column or entrance way overhang supported by a pillar or column may have curb appeal, the main consideration is how does it feel as you exit your front door. Are they too large or too close to the door way? As you exit your home, do you feel caged in? Can you see straight ahead or is your view obstructed and in a similar manner will opportunities coming to you be blocked or diverted?

**Solutions:** If you have porch columns or actual pillars that are oversized or placed to close together, hanging planters or potted plants, vines or other creative solutions like wrapping the pillars or columns with colorful material may break up the cold, unfeeling straight and perpendicular lines and transform it into a more natural and intimate setting.

## 90. Tree trunk, lamp post, telephone or utility pole directly opposite the front door of the house.

A tree trunk, lamp post, telephone or utility pole opposite the front door of a house is not so bad if at least 50 feet away. Closer than 50 feet becomes a serious issue depending on the size of the tree trunk, lamp post, telephone or utility pole. Even a fire hydrant in direct line of the front door can be considered negative depending if it is large enough to appear as an obstacle blocking movement (i.e. ch'i flow) to the front door. Any large object directly in front of the door is not only blocking beneficial ch'i from flowing in but is

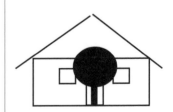

also "attacking" the health and well-being of the inhabitants.

The entrance way as the mouth of the house is symbolic of how the home receives nourishment. Blocking the entrance way of a home is comparable to putting your fist in your mouth and then trying to eat. The magnitude of the difficulties to be anticipated can also be exasperated if the tree trunk, lamp post, telephone or utility pole is at the beginning of a straight walkway leading from the sidewalk/street to the front door.

In some cases the tree is not a straight tree trunk but rather a broad limbed, curling branched tree such as a sycamore or old oak. In these cases the tree trunk "meanders" and is not a "straight arrow" aimed at the door. Even so a massive tree directly in front of the home's entrance way may still block the flow of ch'i. The beauty of the tree may distract from the fact that the ch'i flow is blocked and engender a feeling of isolation and separation from the outside world. Again how far the tree is from the entrance way is crucial in making the decision as to whether the house under consideration is a worthy investment.

**Solutions:** The most obvious first solution, in lieu of removing the tree, street sign, lamp post or utility pole that is "attacking" the front door, is to shield it with a hedge, fence or screen. The next approach would be to decorate with a bird house, bird feeder, wind chime, or strips of colorful fabric (see page 75, #66 - View of a tree trunk, lamp post or utility pole through a window.) Installing two lamp posts on either side of your pathway may, like two sentinels, protect you from the "attacking" tree, lamp post, utility or telephone pole.

### 91. Front entrance recessed or hidden from view.

When we begin any journey, we feel more secure and comfortable when we have knowledge of our destination. When we begin any project, it is encouraging to have a sense of its expected outcome. When we walk the path to our front door and cannot see the front door, we feel uncertainty. Or is a recessed front door an attempt to hide from the busyness of the world? The more difficult it is to find the front door, the more your opportunities will have difficulty finding you. This situation is made all the more difficult if as you step out your front door, you are confronted by a fence or wall.

**Solutions:** This should be easy to overcome by the positioning of "guide posts" along the way. Objects like a bird bath or plantings that are like friends leading us, or any one coming to visit us, down the path guiding us to the front door.

Even from the street, there should be no confusion or hesitation as to where your front door is. Foliage on either side of the front door can give a sense of privacy but the plants should not be overpowering, scratchy (bougainvillea) or in any way obscure the entrance as seen from down the pathway. Additional enhancements might be positioning of the address of the house, a

mailbox or a lawn fountain – all of which draw the eye, and the beneficial ch'i, forward. Hanging a wind chime to "sound forth" and keeping a porch light on all the time to energize the entrance way may also be helpful.

## 92. Overhanging balcony or an excessively large lintel over the front door.

An overhanging second floor balcony over the front door or an excessively large lintel may appear somewhat like a guillotine ready to drop. The appearance of heaviness will translate into blocked opportunities, heaviness of the heart, and ultimately loneliness and despair. (Compare page 68, #55 - Exposed beams and roof supports.)

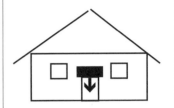

**Solutions:** To avoid the negative effects of an oppressive weight hanging over the front door, decorate to alter the appearance to make it "lighter." This can be done by painting the beam, the ceiling and the walls the same light color as dark against light or light against dark will accentuate the heaviness of the overhang. All-in-all, not a good design element.

## 93. Doorways with glass panels or doorways that look strange.

Doorways come in many designs. Plain and unadorned to elaborate facing. Some look proud, some artsy, some humorous and some exceedingly strange as if left over from a gothic horror movie. Like all shapes and configurations what does the door say about who lives behind it?

**Solutions:** Solid wood is best. All glass is the worst – glass is easily broken and, though elegant, can leave the inhabitants feeling vulnerable and exposed. If the decision is to use a door with glass panels in order to bring light into a dark foyer or hallway, limit the glass to the upper 1/3 of the door and choose a door that appears strong and sturdy, not frail and fragile. And change the clear glass to opaque. Some doors have design motifs which can suit your tastes and others that make you feel uncomfortable. It is not smart to compromise. If the door is strange don't hesitate to change the door and get one you like and that you feel represents your energy and style.

## 94. Front door too large or too small in proportion to the front façade of the house.

If the doorway is too small in relationship to the front façade of the house, identities will feel diminished, resulting in conflicts and discord as individuals try to prove themselves. If the doorway is too large, your good fortune will leak out and there will be unrealistic goals and expenditures.

If a doorway is too small, or if it is too high and too narrow or too low and too wide, our energetic field, often called the aura, will need to contract in order to pass through. This upset to one's electro-magnetic field can be

compared to being "punched" each time you walk through the door. Such a doorway is uninviting. This continual assault is experienced as emotional upset and eventually will lead to health problems as well.

**Solutions:** The doorway should feel comfortable to walk through so we feel neither cramped nor diminished. A proper proportion is at least 12" above and on either side. The primary entranceway to a home should also appear to be in proportion to the design of the home's façade. The front door should be the largest door of the home. When internal doors are larger than the front door, the entranceway will be "consumed" by the larger internal door (page 59, #45, – "Tiger's mouth"). Painting the door and door frame a bright color may give it a larger appearance while darker paint may make a door appear smaller.

### 95. Garage more prominent than the front door.

In older country homes the garage is off to the side and detached from the main house while in many subdivisions where homes are built close to the street with narrow walk ways separating one home from the other, garages are up front and prominent. With two or even three car garages stretching across more than half of the front façade of the home, cars rule. The feng shui challenge is to restore the balance so cars serve and we do not feel "driven." This is even more difficult when the front door is recessed.

**Solution:** Avoid placing additional emphasis on the garage by decorating it or painting it a contrasting color. Add landscaping or fences to diminish its appearance by drawing the eye elsewhere. If the only path to your front door is from the driveway, add another pathway across your lawn using decorative stone or brickwork. A row of low voltage or solar lights can also be used for accenting. Line the path with flowering plants to make it clear where the main door is and that it is the door of greater importance.

### 96. The Ming T'ang - the "bright hall".

The Chinese expression Ming T'ang is loosely translated as the "bright hall" and refers to the openness and sense of uplift that is felt in open spaces in comparison to dark and contracted areas. In regards to your dwelling, this effect of openness is achieved if there is an open space directly in front of the main entrance so that as you open the door you can look outward. The presence of a view translates as having "vision" for creative expression in all areas of life, just as a blocked entrance way, a recessed entrance way or one without any Ming T'ang comes to represent feelings of obstruction in work endeavors, uninspired opportunities and a sense of going nowhere which will further undermine health and harmony in relationships.

**Solutions:** Creating a Ming T'ang in a narrow alley way or where the door opens up facing the side of another building or a fence between dwellings can

be quite difficult. A large Welcome mat in front of the door, any landscaping or potted plants will certainly help. If it is possible to hang a picture or paint a mural on a fence or wall opposite the front door that depicts a scenic panorama. Perhaps the scene can be a landscape or seascape showing a distant horizon. But the best homes to choose have their front doors looking out over a patch of greenery.

## 97. A Ming T'ang inside your home.

As you walk into the home, a Ming T'ang is the feeling of spaciousness and accomplishment that further inspires a joy of life. It gives a place to center oneself before choosing which direction to go. It's a place to "land." Perhaps with a closet to hang your coat, a shelf or side table to put your keys on, and a mirror to the side to enhance the openness and allow you to see how your appearance might be. If the Ming T'ang is a small foyer, do not clutter it.

**Solutions:** You can try to make it appear wider and more spacious by hanging a mirror or framed-picture with glass over the picture to give a sense of expansiveness and depth. It is nice to enhance this sense of centering with an appropriate throw carpet or marble-tiled area. A potted plant or a desk top water fountain may enliven the Ming T'ang. A lead-glass crystal sphere hanging on a nine-inch red ribbon to add some sparkle. Avoid putting clutter or your monthly bills on a side table with a mirror above it. Remember, mirrors double whatever is in front of them, and you do not want to double your clutter or the money you owe.

## 98. Narrow hallway leading from the front door into the house

A narrow hallway leading from the front door into the house that is only wide enough for one person to walk along symbolizes unhappiness in relationships and a person who lives alone or feels alone. Unless there are some other more supportive factors, this house will not allow two people to walk and live together without contention and constant argument.

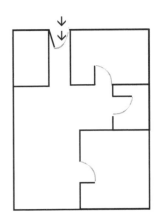

**Solutions:** This configuration needs remodeling. It may be possible to widen the hallway using mirrors as long as hanging mirrors or pictures on the wall won't be bumped against making these remedies no better than worthless clutter. If remodeling is impossible or too costly, and the hallway too narrow to widen with mirrors and pictures, avoid this house. It will only bring unhappiness.

## 99. Small foyer with a wall opposite the front door.

It's amazing how the human psychology gets agitated and tightens up in preparation for a struggle when first confronted by an obstacle. Perhaps it is

91

less amazing, and certainly sad, how the human psychology begins to despair when confronted by the same obstacle time and time again. Staring at a blank wall forces us to turn within which might be appropriate when we wish to meditate or be self observing but certainly is depressing and undermining to one's self confidence and self assertiveness. Even our posture will begin to stoop in despair at the inability to overcome this obstacle.

**Solutions:** A small foyer with a wall opposite the front door lowers vitality as soon as we open the door, unless there is something to entertain the eye. Depending on how close the wall is to the door depends on how to decorate it. The guideline is to hang a picture that is uplifting in its color and symbology and one that gives the eye a sense of depth of field. Consider land- or water-scapes that provide a distant view.

You do not want to use a mirror for this purpose as has been suggested by more than one author. That suggestion is based on a mirror's use in making things disappear as it provides the illusion of looking through something. Unfortunately, a mirror at the front door operates differently. As you open the door and look into a mirror only a few feet from your face, you become startled as you suddenly see your image looking back at you. The first reaction is that of bouncing energy back at you and with that the mirror bounces incoming ch'i (your money) right back out again.

If the foyer is large enough perhaps there could be a side table with a bowl of fresh flowers or a table top water fountain to energize the entrance way. Water fountains that flow in a direction are preferred to a 360° fountain. The fountain should be positioned with the water flowing in the direction of the rest of the home and not flowing in the direction of the front door. You want money flowing into the house and not out to the neighborhood.

A small area rug is also suggested as mentioned above, (page 91, #97 - A Ming T'ang inside your home). Blank walls represent obstacles and give a feeling of isolation and then confusion leading to breakdowns and emotional unravelling. In short, a wall to close to the front door stifles chi and one's chances for growth. Tie bells to your door knob.

### 100. Split-wall as you enter.

A split-wall upon entering a house results in a left brain-right brain imbalance as one eye sees depth and the other has to adapt to a closer point of focus. The resultant strain lowers vitality and may contribute to persistent headaches or nerve related disorders.

**Solutions:** Evaluate carefully if remedies can be put in place or if the area is too tight and any remedies would add to the confusion. The challenge here is to restore balance. This can be done by either adding a plant, statue, wind chime or other hanging attraction to bring the distance view into the fore-

ground, or, visa versa, by hanging a framed-picture of a landscape or some distant view covered with glass to give the illusion of depth and of looking into the distance.

## 101. Beam inside across the hall or foyer near the front door.

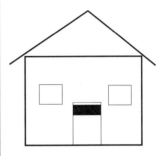

Beams are not favored architectural features as they are usually weight-bearing and therefore "feel" heavy exerting a down-pushing force. Beams also break the otherwise smooth, unobstructed ch'i flow across a ceiling resulting in a "choppy" flow or a life of obstacles and barriers to overcome. As pointed out, people tend to avoid sitting under a beam (page 68, #55), and have problems sleeping under a beam (page 106, #118).

It should be obvious that upon walking through the front door of a home being confronted by a beam, especially one that is fairly low will be "felt" as a bump in the head. The good ch'i that enters through the front door will become trapped with a general feeling of depression permeating the mood of the home. Once again if this is the only major problem than it isn't too serious. However, if this is one of many such problems consider finding a home that is less obstructed.

**Solutions:** At least paint the beam the same color as the ceiling itself. Obviously a dark color against a light ceiling will accentuate the negative. If the beam is high enough, you might consider painting the ceiling with a faux finish such as a cloud-like effect to give the illusion that the beam is not even there.

The more traditional cure for a beam is hanging two bamboo flutes some-where along the beam to break the straight line and alter the down pushing appearance to one of meandering. With this in mind almost any decorations – playful masks from other cultures or hand-painted flowering tendrils – will successfully mitigate the oppressiveness of a beam by allowing the ch'i to sym-bolically flow through it. If the beam is low and you are tall, the illusion of making it disappear will be more difficult to achieve. Curtains, swags and cornices are other alternative decorative countermeasures.

## 102. Back door or window opposite the front door.

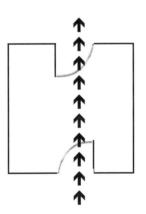

This is an important problem that some authorities feel can not be rem-edied. An often it cannot. Especially when the back door or window are in very close proximity to the front door – perhaps with only a foyer separating the two, or when the back windows are very large or sliding glass doors.

Homes that are built in this manner often have a lovely view or backyard garden to show off. In some situations the ch'i can be evaluated as "captured" by the garden and sent back but usually the ch'i just "flies away." Even with two rooms in between, the in-coming ch'i (health and money) tends to "race" straight through the house in the line of least resistance.

**Solutions:** To keep the ch'i from racing through the house and going out the back window or door, curtain the doorway and back window. Also consider ways to slow down or deflect the flow of ch'i as it comes through the front door and heads to the back of the house.

If there is a sliding glass door opposite the front door, positioning potted plants behind the fixed glass side will help to catch the eye and the ch'i as the front door opens and the ch'i heads for the rear of the house. Placing wind chimes near the back door will also help. A properly positioned screen may be appropriate but be careful not to obstruct the movement of people through this area. In some cases the proper placement of cures and the actual dimensions of the space between the front door and back door is quite adequate while in other situations it is a case of using a band-aid to cover a gaping wound. The challenge is to get the nourishing ch'i to flow from the front door throughout the rest of the house. Be careful with this one.

Hang attractive things in the window such as a lead-glass crystal sphere(s) to diffuse the ch'i. Or hang a sun catcher with pressed flowers or a stained-glass ornament, or some other attractive piece to catch the exiting ch'i, gather it up, and send it back to you so as you cross the threshold you do not feel/sense your personal ch'i taking the" path of least resistance" and flowing out the back window. Lead-glass crystal spheres or wind chimes can also be hung from the ceiling midway between the front and back of the house.

Hollow tube wind chimes are used to conduct the in-coming ch'i upward slowing its momentum plus they are harmonious to hear, and even to see, they symbolize harmony. Choose a small wind chime that does not feel like its a chunk of metal falling from the ceiling. It should be hung high enough and be small enough to be unobtrusive. how obtrusive it can be depends on the height of the ceiling relative to the size of the wind chime and perhaps to a greater part by the kind of wind chime you have chosen. Are they whimsical? Nostalgic? Do they have an Oriental motif? Do not get wind chimes that look like heavy silver tubes that could hurt you as you walked beneath them.

Putting a carpet on the floor or putting a small table with flowers under the back window will also slow the ch'i flow down while sending back uplifting positive energies.

### 103. Stairway facing the front door.

If there is a stairway from an upper floor leading directly down to the entrance way, this too will have a negative impact on health and prosperity as all the good ch'i upstairs flows down the stairs and out the door.

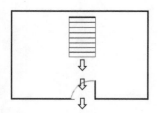

**Solutions:** If the stairway cannot be remodeled so the last two or three steps face away from the front door, you can try installing as many cures as possible: placing a small throw rug between the bottom of the stairs and the front door; hanging a 30mm lead-glass crystal sphere from the ceiling on a red

ribbon midway between the door and the stairs; positioning a potted plant off to the side of the bottom step; and installing a runner carpet with a meandering pattern to slow the ch'i down and make it easier to go up and down the stairs. Pictures on the wall of the stairway will also help to "lift" the ch'i up the stairs while slowing the ch'i coming down the stairs. This is another situation that is best avoided if possible.

### 104. Stairway going up and another going down – "Mandarin duck."

A point of focus is needed when we come in the front door. This can be achieved by hanging a large painting or art print, having a statue or a group of potted plants. When the eye is greeted by a diversity of images or structural components competing for attention, confusion results. This then is the guideline for dealing with split-walls or any other entrance way situation that lacks a unified point of focus including the stairway situation with one set of stairs going down while the other goes up like the wings of a "Mandarin duck." Balance is thrown off and ultimately the immune system is undermined by the stress and the inability to rectify or adapt restfully to the stress producing situation.

**Solutions:** The challenge is to create a stronger foreground to focus on. In the case of a stairway going up and another going down, you have to answer the question: which way is the ch'i flowing? and accentuate that direction. This can be done by painting that stairwell with a brighter color, or perhaps having a runner carpet with a stronger pattern. If there is space enough between the two doorways, a potted plant might be positioned to stabilize the ch'i flow. If there is enough space, a painting, print or some other wall-hanging might draw the eye to it before the mind is split with having to make the decision to choose to go up or down. Hanging a faceted lead-glass crystal prism and having an area carpet (page 91, #97 – Ming T'ang) would also be helpful.

Evaluate a "Mandarin duck" split-stairway situation carefully as it can be quite critical to your focus and ultimately to your well-being.

### 105. Stairway at street level leads down into the main living area of the home.

Coming into a home on an upper level and then having to walk down a few steps is not as unstable if you have to walk down several or even a whole flight of stairs. The steeper the stairway the more uneasy the psyche feels. What if I lose my balance? What if I fall? Younger more agile individuals are less likely to feel insecure but even those who are usually more surefooted are likely to experience that moment of hesitation, that momentary fear of falling forward, that translates to the subconscious as unsteadiness, uncertainty and lack of confidence. All of which correlates to the "action" of going to a lower level which may translate into life as demotion or difficulty getting support from others.

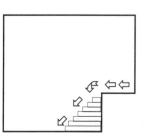

**Solutions:** Evaluate how narrow, wide, high and steep the staircase is. If you feel trepidation or even vertigo just looking down the stairs, look to buy or rent elsewhere. If the staircase isn't too steep, the ceiling high, and the walls set wide apart, some adjustments can be applied. Similar to a sunken living room or any sunken room where balance is distorted, consider a runner carpet to soften one's steps and give more traction to convey firmness and certainty.

Perhaps you can also put some lights along either side as they do in a movie theater or even a day-glo strip along the edge to clearly demarcate each step. If the stairs are wide enough, potted plants or objects on each step can also help define the height and width of the step so the mind can quickly adjust to the descending sequence of surfaces. Appropriately positioned decorations can break up the fast downward moving ch'i by giving the eye things to focus on. All these ideas can also be applied to any staircase going from one floor to another.

### 106. Bathroom above the front entrance way.

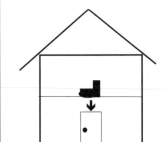

Bathroom ch'i is considered negative as it is associated with body waste and the toilet with flushing waste down. The Bathroom-Toilet consequently becomes a negative symbol to have over the front door of a home. Even when not thinking of the fact that the bathroom is overhead as you cross the threshold of your home, the subconscious/emotional body "feels" the bathroom-toilet-waste-flushing imagery without a doubt. And where is the waste going once it is flushed? Find out if the pipes are plumbed to go along side the doorway possibly emitting odors or distracting sounds.

**Solutions:** Tough one to solve as the symbolic reality is what it is: bathroom over doorway – "body waste overhead." One cure is to install a mirror on the inside of the entrance way that faces upward reflecting the bathroom ch'i away. Some might suggest a small wind chime preferably with a pagoda on top – the kind you would have to go to Chinatown to buy – but any wind chime will do that you find aesthetically pleasing.

The wind chimes should not be too large nor too small, and not hanging so low that people might hit their head or even come close to brushing through their hair. The right balance is somewhere in there. If you find that right balance, a wind chime inside the front door directly under the bathroom hanging from the ceiling will not seem obtrusive. The wind chime represents harmony and the desired harmonics of personal relationships. Wind chimes have tubes that conduct ch'i flow upward.

With this in mind, hang the wind chime to reverse the flow of negative down pushing ch'i and channel good ch'i upward and bring one thoughts to harmony as members of the household cross the threshold entering their abode with positive, uplifting vibrations.

### 107. Bathroom by or opposite the front door.

A bathroom located immediately by the front entrance way or bathroom door opposite the entrance way will result in great misfortune as the ch'i of the house (health and money) will come in the front door and immediately go down the toilet.

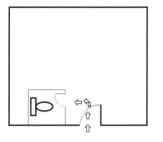

**Solutions:** In either of these cases, cures need to be installed immediately and it would be best to avoid homes with these configurations. Remember, what you see is what you get, so opening the front door should reveal a positive uplifting image and not one of bathrooms and waste. If you cannot avoid such a home or until you find another, at least keep the bathroom doors closed at all times. It would be wise to mount a mirror on the bathroom door to deflect the ch'i away from the bathroom.

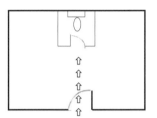

### 108. Kitchen first room you see from the front door.

The first room seen gets all the attention. As mentioned in #100 above, the bathroom is the worst room to have next to the entrance way. The foyer is probably the best and a living room the next best. Whichever room is first tends to be the one that preoccupies the thoughts of the inhabitants, especially when they come home. As a home shapes its inhabitants, even before coming home, the thoughts turn to the first room to be entered. If it is the bedroom, the desire is to take a nap. If it is a den or study, the desire is to be alone. If it is the living room and the television is visible from the door, the temptation is to turn it on. If the stairs, the desire is to run up stairs and hide in one's room inclining family members to feel isolated from each other.

If the kitchen is near the door, thoughts most naturally turn to food. What's for dinner? Is there going to be enough dessert? What will I have for breakfast? If the refrigerator is in prominent view, the door will open frequently. Food issues, weight, and diet may dominate household conversations.

**Solutions:** If there is a kitchen by the front door, consider keeping the door closed. If there is no door, consider a curtain and some other placement of a wall-hanging or floor decoration that will draw your eye and your attention away from the kitchen and into the living area of the dwelling.

### 109. Stove or fireplace can be seen from the front door.

In olden days of wood burning stoves a stove in direct line of the front door could easily be blown out or cooled by a door opening and a breeze blowing in. Though we no longer use a wood burning stove, still a breeze cools the food cooking. Perhaps more significant is the prosperity symbol of the stove and that seeing it from the front door is perceived as an "attack" or a dissipation of the home's prosperity. A breeze can also cool a fire in the fireplace but the main problem is the ch'i coming in going up right up the flue.

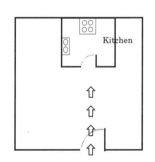

**Solutions:** The most obvious solution in lieu of moving the stove or fireplace out of direct sight of the front door is to hang a curtain or put up a tri-fold screen which offers a decorative motif to those who stand at the front door blocking the view of the more intimate areas of family activities.

### 110. Entrance of an apartment next to or opposite an elevator.

With the constant activity that an elevator implies, and the on and off whirring of its motor, an apartment next to or opposite an elevator generates unstable feelings of uncertainty. Finances and health no doubt will constantly be "moving up and down." In addition to the changing circumstances of the elevator, there is also the continual distraction from the flow of people coming and going. An apartment adjacent to an elevator shaft results in even more difficulties for its inhabitants as the noise is louder and the conscious awareness of the shaft as a dangerous place generates fears.

**Solutions:** Mirrors can be used to push the elevator energy away and potted plants or heavy furniture can be used as a stabilizing force. Best of all is to avoid apartments next to or opposite an elevator unless the elevator solely serves your apartment as the only apartment on your floor.

*The Dragon & the Phoenix represent relationship harmony.*

**Chinese paper cutting folk art.**

# Rest, Rejuvenation and Romance
## Evaluating the Bedroom

The secret of the home and womb is one.
~~ Dennis Fairchild, *Healing Home: Feng Shui Then & Now*

The bedroom should be a place of rest, rejuvenation and romance with a sense of security and quiet. The condition of the bedroom is more than just that it is kept clean with dusted furniture, washed windows, and a made bed with fresh sheets. The bedroom needs to be a place that feels secure so sleep is undisturbed. This means the bedroom needs to be quiet throughout the night. As a place of rest and rejuvenation, a bedroom with good feng shui is as important as having a good front door. It is best located toward the back of the house away from activity where it can fulfill its purpose of providing rest with a feeling of protection.

As others have pointed out, the bedroom is where we spend one-third of our lives. Our transitions from waking to dream realms and back again should be undisturbed and as pleasant as possible. The bedroom should be a sanctuary, a safe haven, and a wonderful environment for intimacy and romance. A lot of thought should go into creating the best bedroom-feng shui possible.

The quality of our sleep is as important as the quality of our food. Just as poor quality food (containing pesticides, chemical food additives, preservatives and food coloring, radiated, genetically modified, overly cooked, microwaved, etc.) will undermine health and result in health problems, so too, poor quality sleep will ultimately undermine health and vitality.

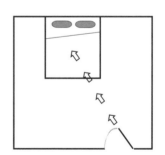

A bedroom overcrowded with furniture can be subconsciously perceived as a hostile environment – to many sharp edges and angles to battle upon entering or leaving. Even the edge of the bedroom door should not be left partial open if it will be pointing at the bed. To many mirrors in a bedroom can be energizing as light bounces around the room. Uncurtained windows can lack intimacy.

The bedroom needs to be a quiet place without noise with a pleasant arrangement of shapes, colors and textures. Sleeping on a solid bed, with a good quality mattress, and comfortable pillows, surrounded by pleasant colors, shapes, textures and images is a pre-requisite. Remove all clutter from

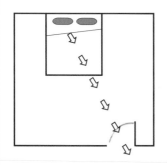

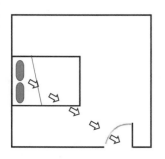

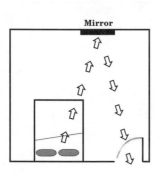

Mirror

around and beneath the bed so ch'i can flow freely around you as you sleep. If the bedroom has a desk or exercise equipment, use a screen to separate these activities from the activity of sleep. From the bed it would also be nice to look out the window at a pleasant view of natural surroundings especially a view of water as water symbolizes abundance, nourishment, good luck and inspiration.

## 111. Bed in the Command Position.

In evaluating the bedroom the first and most important factor is the positioning of the bed. In considering which wall to put the bed on there may be pre-existing conditions that limit your choosing the best direction. Obviously the bed cannot be against a wall with closet doors along it.

**Solutions:** Ideally, you want your your headboard to be against a solid wall with the widest possible view of the whole room. This is called the Command Position.

The Command Position allows you to see the door and anyone coming through it. The Command Position also allows you to see the greatest area of the room while lying or sitting in bed without having to turn your head to the left or right. When you sit at your desk or lie in your bed, the Command Position gives you the greatest sense of security and therefore of restfulness.

The Command Position is primarily about our need to feel secure, seeing and anticipating what is coming our way. Consider if you were a New York City mobster in a restaurant, would you sit with your back to the door? Probably not. It is interesting to note that when a couple goes to a restaurant it is almost guaranteed that the man will choose the Command Position with his "weaker" friend taking the more vulnerable position of having her back to the door and being dependent on the "man" to protect her. The Command Position puts you in the driver's seat – it puts you in control of any situation.

In evaluating your bedroom, if you cannot arrange your bed to be in the Command Position consider if it is possible to position a mirror on the wall opposite the door that will allow you to see if anyone is coming in. A mirror properly placed is just like a rear view mirror which keeps a driver in a car in control by letting him or her know what's going on behind their back. Instead of a mirror, any reflective surface will suffice. Once installed, the sense of security – that is, being able to see the door and sense what is going on in the rest of the house – allows comfort, relaxation and relationship harmony to return to the bedroom.

Avoid putting your bed at an angle to the wall or with a corner of the room behind the headboard. A solid wall gives the best support while a bed floating in the middle of the room or turned at an angle to the wall symbolizes chaos and confusion. A bed positioned with a solid wall behind, with a commanding view of the largest area of the room is also the most aesthetically pleasing.

## 112. Door directly in front of the foot of the bed – the Coffin Position.

When the entrance to the bedroom is directly in front of the bed, it is called the Coffin Position. According to my mother, my great grandmother from eastern Europe also alluded to this placement of the bed as the Coffin Position. Apparently she said, "This is the way they carry you out – feet first."

Avoid this placement at all costs. This situation is made worse if there is a bathroom door opposite the bedroom door, a bathroom or electronic devices on the other side of the wall from the headboard, a window directly behind the headboard, or if the ceiling is sloped over the bed, or if there is a beam overhead. Any one of these situations is detrimental and even more so if the bed itself is positioned in direct line of the door.

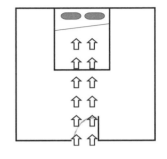

Death is implied by this bed position due to the continual stress of the individual sleeping with their feet to the door. A night or two or even three will not bear such a terminal fate. But certainly after years, the continual anticipation of danger, the '"what if something came crashing through the door-how can I protect myself" kind of fear and uncertainty, and the all-night activation of the "fight or flight" adrenal glands will take its toll on the immune system.

**Solutions:** Any solution other than moving the bed is inadequate. Temporary measures can be considered until the bed is moved; and, if the the bed can not be moved, the only solution is to move to another house.

To temporarily off-set the feelings of vulnerability the most obvious solution is to close the door. At least this gives a moment, were the door to open suddenly by an attacker, to pull oneself together in time to confront the intruder. Not much time and perhaps not time enough but at least there is a delay that may work in one's favor. In other words there might be a little more restfulness but perhaps still too much anticipation of danger.

Some practitioners may also suggest cures such as hanging a wind chime inside the room between the doorway and the bed to draw the incoming excessive ch'i flow upwards. Others may suggest a throw carpet between the foot of the bed and the doorway, a hope chest and at least a foot board on the bed. But I repeat these are merely band-aids and can not be taken seriously. Move the bed or move to another house.

## 113. Doorways on either side of the bed.

Another undermining influence to avoid is doorways on either side of the bed. Whether it is the door you enter the bedroom through or bathroom doors or doors that lead to an outside porch or garden setting, doors on either side of the bed are not healthy. We never want to position a bed, desk or major sitting or working area in direct line of the entrance way into a room as that would be similar to sitting all day on "railroad tracks" waiting to be broadsided.

Deep relaxation is not enhanced by knowing we could be taken by surprise.
~~ Nancilee Wydra,
*Feng Shui: the Book of Cures*

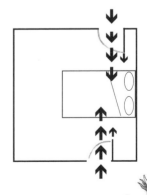

Doorways to either side of the bed are also discomforting. Whomever sleeps on the side of the bed with a doorway on that side, will tend to feel more vulnerable and sleep less deeply with anticipation of someone or something barging in unexpectedly. With a door way to either side of the bed or straight ahead translates as sleeping in readiness of an attack or having to handle an unexpected emergency. Trying to sleep while continually being prepared wears away at the immune system which needs sleep to replenish and regenerate. The nervous tension in anticipation and apprehension wears down a person's resistance thus effecting relationship harmony and personal health. The closer the door is to the side of the bed the more intense the stress and the more severe the health issues.

The human body can handle stress for short periods of time. Like waking in the night to walk or feed a baby but then the day arrives when the baby sleeps through the night and the parents return to normal sleep routines. But if normal is never the situation, or when stress becomes the norm, the adrenals keep pumping those "fight and flight" hormones which speeds up the heart beat, raises the blood pressure high, accelerates the breathing, and generates heightened anxiety. With this night-time stress what else can be expected but a lower threshold of tolerance to irritating and irksome situations with ever increasing uptightness and hostile over reactions even to petty situations. If sleep is ruined, the rest of the day is a continuing disaster.

If it is the entrance to the bedroom that is closer to the bed, it is the man who usually chooses that side. Sleeping closer to the door allows the man to "feel in control" of potential emergency situations. He assumes the position to be ready and alert to protect his mate or to be ready to jump to attentiveness if there is trouble elsewhere in the house. Men like to feel like they are in control in the event of an unexpected or out-of-control situation. Invariably the wife, who can comfortably sleep behind the man's protective readiness, remains healthy and strong. In time he falls seriously ill and she becomes the caretaker to the man as he can no longer stem the onslaught of ch'i flowing at him and over him. She continues to take care of him as he feebly attempts to remain in readiness guarding the bedroom door.

If it is a bathroom door to the side of the bed, it is more likely to be the woman who will choose that side either due to her more frequent need or the man's willingness to give the lady the convenience. (Of course an older man may also have to be closer to the bathroom if he has not been taking care of his prostate.) This situation is made even worse if the master bath is *en suite* and lacks a closing door but is connected with an archway or a pocket door that is difficult to close and remains open.

Bathroom ch'i is cooler and yin in comparison to the warmer yang energy of the bedroom, and the two do not mix very well. Sleeping is a restful or yin activity. People are vulnerable when they sleep and that is why the bedroom

needs to be quiet and undisturbed from either outside intrusion or intrusion from interior features such as an overhead beam, "hidden arrows" emanating from furniture, or the extreme yin energy of the bathroom which "drains" out the warm yang energy of the bedroom.

More often than not the individual sleeping closest to the bathroom door will soon succumbs to urinary or bladder problems or gain weight from water retention. How close the door is to the side of the bed and whether it can be closed or curtained are variables that might make this a more tolerable situation. Considering the constitutional strength of the individual sleeping near the bathroom door is of course one of the determining factors as to how soon before health problems manifest or if they can be adequately avoided. For the most part this is not a favorable arrangement and is one to avoid.

**Solutions:** The best solution is to move the bed out of the doorway. If this is not feasible, then evaluate how close to the door way the bed actually is – five feet is very close, eight to ten feet may begin to be far enough. The only measurement tool that is dependable is your own feelings. If you can't convince yourself that you are too close or far enough away, ask a friend or family member whose intuition, or so-called feeling judgement, you can trust.

As with many situations such as this, a 40mm lead-glass crystal prism can be hung on a nine-inch red ribbon between the entrance to the bathroom and the toilet. The crystal will diffuse the in-coming positive ch'i and keep it from "going down" the toilet. A small throw rug can be placed between the door and the bed to slow the ch'i down. It is also suggested that all bathroom doors are kept closed to keep auspicious ch'i/money from going down the toilet. And don't forget to keep your toilet seat closed for the same reason.

As with the Coffin Position described above (page 100, #112), solutions, other than moving the bed to a better arrangement, are at best temporary until you find a home offering a better bedroom configuration. Needless to say, at least close the door. Unlike the Coffin Position or the entrance to the bedroom along side the bed, with a bathroom entrance, security isn't the primary issue. In this case a closed bathroom door keeps the warm bedroom ch'i from being dissipated by the cool, damp bathroom ch'i.

When pocket doors are awkward and hard to use, they are usually left open. To encourage closing the door, I suggest getting a draw pull or cabinet handle to attach to the very edge of the door so when it is open, the draw pull or cabinet handle keeps the door from being completely pushed inside its pocket. Then it is easy to close the door and the tendency to leave it open will be averted. If the bathroom is *en suite,* a curtain rod can be installed and curtains that can be pulled shut can be hung.

But best of all move the bed out of the doorway. Either move the bed to another acceptable position in the room, or use another room, or find another house.

### 114. Toilet in direct line with the bed.

As Master Peter Leung has so astutely pointed out, the toilet itself "radiates" negative ch'i both forward and back. Looking at a floor plan should make it quite clear if the front or back of the toilet is in direct line with where a bed will be positioned. Negative toilet ch'i is usually associated with ill-health and ill-health will eventually undermine relationship harmony and or career success. The part of the body most clearly in direct line of the toilet ch'i is the area of the body most likely to manifest a particular ailment though the toilet ch'i can have a detrimental effect on the immune system itself. Do not under estimate the seriousness of negative toilet ch'i. A toilet in direct line with the bedroom door is just as inauspicious and will also bring ill-health to those who sleep with this configuration.

**Solution:** Whether the bathroom is connected to the bedroom or situated elsewhere in the house, the bed should be shielded from the toilet by placing at least a 24" x 30-36" mirror behind or in front of the toilet to reflect the toilet energy back onto itself. The mirror can be positioned in the bathroom itself or on the other side of the wall from the toilet in the adjoining room. If the mirror is being place in the adjoining room, it can be placed behind a piece of furniture or in a closet – but be sure to place with the mirrored-side facing the front or back of the toilet. In the bedroom this remedy is only necessary if the front or back of the toilet is in direct line with a sleeping arrangement. If there is a toilet in direct line of the bedroom door, find a different bedroom to sleep in. If there is a door opposite the bedroom door, at least keep the bathroom door closed and place some decorative art on the door itself.

### 115. Headboard on the other side of the wall from a bathroom.

The problem with a bathroom on the other side of the wall from the headboard is how the plumbing with water in and moving through the pipes will effect a sleeping body. The most likely health complaints will also be related to the kidneys, urinary tract or lymphatic system. If the bathroom is on the other side of the wall from the headboard but the plumbing is not in the wall the headboard is on, the physical problems will be somewhat mitigate however the effect on one's psychology will still be disturbed.

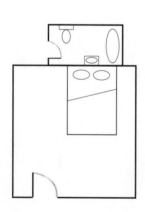

Even worse is when the house electrical system is grounded to the water pipes instead of a six foot rebar pounded down into the earth. If this is the case then the whole house is electrified and the water pipes in the wall behind the bed become a conduit for electrical energy emanating an electro-magnetic field making the water pipes in the wall behind the bed even more detrimental to health and well-being. Even without water pipes in the wall behind the bed, this is still a very negative situation as the water pipes will still be generating a massive electro-magnetic field throughout the home.

**Solutions:** The best solution of course is to move the bed to a different wall. If this can not be accomplished, as with negative toilet ch'i, the only real solution is to place a mirror between the headboard and the wall with the mirrored surface facing the bathroom which should deflect the bathroom energy away from the bed. But this is another of those situations that are best avoided.

If the house electrical system is grounded to the water pipes, disconnect and have the electrical system ground to an six foot rebar pounded into the earth.

## 116. Electric box, electric devices, or stove on the other side of the wall from a bed.

Three case histories should help illustrate the severity of this problem. One involved a contractor who bought, renovated and sold homes and often lived in the homes he was renovating while he did the work and until the home was sold. This home renovator developed arhythmic heart condition within weeks of moving into the master bedroom suite. After it was pointed out that the incoming electric boxes was attached to the house within twenty-feet of the headboard, he changed rooms and his heart condition disappeared immediately much to the doctor's surprise.

The other case history is of a woman with progressively worsening cancer of the ovaries which developed soon after moving into her parent's house after the woman's mother had passed away from a similar cancerous condition. After his wife's death, the father decided he would be happy in the smaller guest house toward the back of the property and invited his daughter and son-in-law to live in the main house, thinking this would be a benefit for them having a larger house without a mortgage and for him having his family close by.

The bed in the master bedroom was in the same position as the parent's bed. On examining the bedroom it was observed that the headboard was on the other side of the wall from the master bathroom and although the wall had no pipes in it, there was a wall heater with heavy electrical conduit running right behind the headboard. The woman's cancerous condition rapidly improved once she began sleeping in a different room. The home was eventually sold and the couple purchased a home with a better bedroom situation. It should also be noted that there was a huge weeping willow in the front yard signaling that this was a home with great sadness.

The third story is of a young couple who hadn't been sleeping in the same bed for quite some. He slept on the living room couch and she slept on the edge of her bed. Looking outside the bedroom window, I saw the electric wires from the transformer can on the utility pole stretching across their backyard to the power box bolted to the outside wall on the other side of the headboard just to the right of the side of the bed no one was sleeping in.

**Solutions:** Move the bed to a different room or at least do not sleep near an electro-magnetic field until you find another house. This also would include sleeping with a refrigerator on the other side of the wall, electric blankets left plugged in the wall all night long, telephone and answer machine AC to DC transformer boxes plugged into the wall beneath your head, and so forth.

Reduce your exposure to electro-magnetic fields whenever and however you can. Considering that your blood cells are like little bar magnets and are all lined up in a row as they flow through your blood stream – plus/minus, plus/minus, plus/minus. Add an electro-magnetic field and the bar magnets spin around, not functioning as they were intended to function and under-mining the blood's ability to nourish the body by transporting vitamins, minerals, proteins, hormones, enzymes, and other components necessary for the proper functioning of the body and mind.

### 117. An irregular-shaped bedroom.

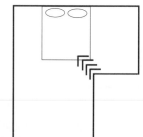

The human mind has a constant need to create order and regularity out of chaos and discord, which is why the square and the rectangle have come to symbolize regularity, dependability and stability. A house that has an irregular-shape has no easily discernible center, a front room that runs in different directions can lack focus, and like-wise an irregular-shaped bedroom can make those using that room feel out of balance.

**Solutions:** The primary challenge is to block the "hidden arrow" coming off any corners created by irregular-shape rooms, especially if the arrow is pointing directly at the doorway, sitting area, stove or bed. In one irregularly shaped bedroom we lived in, in addition to hanging a 40mm faceted lead-glass crystal sphere as a protection, my wife covered the edge with a gossa-mer scarf that replaced the aggressive edge with a splash of color. Tacking up molding on the edge is another way to round the edge and transform it into a softer, less aggressive form.

In large rooms of the house a potted plant can also be used to block the corners of walls, pillars or exposed structural supports. In the bedroom plants have to be used with care. During the day while photosynthesis is operating, plants breathe carbon dioxide and exhale oxygen; but at night, the process is reversed and plants compete with humans for oxygen while exhal-ing carbon dioxide.

### 118. Beam over the bed (compare page 68, #55 – Exposed beams and roof supports).

Think twice about choosing a house with beams in the bedroom and be careful about your evaluation as to the possibility of finding a true solution and not just a band-aid. Beams usually cross the bed in one of two ways: horizontally or vertically.

If the beam above a bed crosses the bed from side-to-side, or vertically from corner-to-corner, the area of the body directly under will be weakened. One couple had a beam over their bed which went over their hips and midriff. The wife had sprained her hip in an aerobics class. Nothing particularly remarkable about that except that it was already two years later and the hip was still inflamed. She had tried everything to overcome the inflammatory condition of the hip and pelvis. Concurrently, her partner, a much more emotional type, had developed stomach cramping and was eventually diagnosed with Irritable Bowel Syndrome. This symptom also resisted the attempts of the best healers they could find. Once they understood the role the massive beam over their bed was playing in their discomfort and discontent, they covered the beam and within weeks they each had complete recoveries.

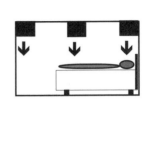

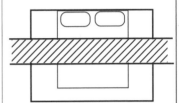

Beams, if aligned vertically over the middle of the bed, will result in partners feeling separated and alienated from each other while a beam directly over one or other of the partners will result in that individual feeling oppressed and eventually succumbing to a major illness. I say this with certainty only because it has been true in every situation that I have observed and is mentioned by every other teacher and in every other book: beams over beds result in serious problems.

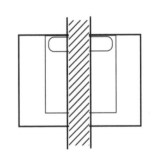

**Solutions:** The best solution for beams in the bedroom is to cover them by completing the ceiling. This can be done with drywall, plywood or, if you like the gypsy encampment look, fabric. As mentioned on page 68, #55 – Exposed beams and roof supports, the negative impact of beams in other areas of the house can possibly be diminished by painting the beams the same color as the rest of the ceiling.

Painting a beam the same color as the rest of the ceiling helps blend them in and upward. Using any of the faux finishes to create a dappled cloud-like effect can also camouflage a beam and diminish the beams oppressive, down-pushing feeling. While beams painted a contrasting color, dark color beams against a white background or white painted beams with a dark background, accentuate the intensity of the beam's appearance.

Hanging two bamboo flutes or several decorations on the beam will alter the unnaturalness of a beam's long straight lines. Any or all of these solutions might work especially if the beams are small and high above. Some times the only solution is to move the bed. But the best beam is no beam at all – especially over the bed.

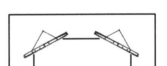

**119. Sloped-ceiling over the bed (compare page 69, #57 – Sloped-ceiling over sitting areas).**

If the head of the bed is on the wall with a sloped-ceiling, the ch'i moving along the ceiling comes down rapidly, causing discomfort and giving some people chronic headaches and others constant neck and shoulder tension.

**Solutions:** As mentioned on page 69, #57 – Sloped-ceiling over sitting area, it is usually adequate to hang a bamboo flute with the mouth piece down and the other end pointing up at a 45° angle to reverse the negative influences of a sloped-ceiling. Two flutes may be stronger than one if the slope is directly over the bed with each flute angled inward. Larger bamboo flutes with theeir thicker walls and notches are stronger than flutes made from reeds.

If the traditional bamboo flutes cure does not fit your interior design style then you are challenged to find a design element that can serve the same purpose. The size of the room and height of the ceiling also needs to be taken into consideration in evaluating the severity of the problem. Using wall-paper border trim at the bottom of the slope around the whole room can help bring intimacy to an otherwise large empty space.

Having the ceiling sloping across the bed may be more difficult for the partner sleeping on the side of the bed closest to the low end of the slope, while sleeping on the wall opposite the low end may foster feelings of criticism for the partner who appears to be squashed and overwhelmed. Either way intimacy is compromised and emotional well-being undermined. Flutes or some other upward pointing objects or wall-hangings may off-set this obvious imbalance.

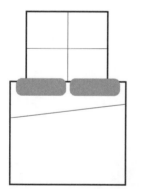

### 120. Bed under a window.

If the only position for the bed is under a window, rest will be disturb by the subconscious concerning itself with the possibility of the window breaking especially if you live in earthquake country or where the winds blow especially strong. Noises from the outside may also seem louder. A window behind a bed means no support.

**Solutions:** A solid wall behind the bed it best. This is another application of the Arm Chair metaphor discussed earlier. A solid wall and a headboard provide comfort. If there is no solid wall on which to position the bed, at least put a heavy curtain on the window that can be closed at night to provide the subconscious with its need for safety and its ability to rest without distraction. A lead-glass crystal sphere and protective images would also be helpful.

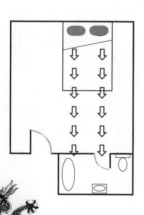

### 121. View from the bed into the bathroom.

Another major consideration is what each individual is seeing from his/her side of the bed. If one person is looking into the bathroom and one is looking at a beautiful view out the window or at a serene painting on the wall, each individual will be preoccupied with different thoughts and the couple's conversations will reflect this reality. One will be talking about vision and dreams while the other will talk about how "crappy" life is, moaning about problems and complaints.

**Solutions:** As you evaluate the bedroom consider if the bed will be in the Command Position without a door on either side, and if the view can be harmonious and uplifting. If one side of the bed looks into the bathroom and the bed can not be repositioned to another wall with a potentially better view, beside keeping the bathroom door closed, consider a wall-hanging or other ways to decorate the doorway itself. How about a wall mural with the door imbedded into the design.

### 122. Master bedroom in front half of house, or extended out in front of the house.

The back portion of the house should be the safest, most intimate and least disturbed by street noise, headlights, etc. A home with the master bedroom in front of the mid-line of the house can weaken a relationship. If the master bedroom in fact is in an extension in front of the house, this can be very detrimental to the relationship as it puts the couple figuratively, and then literally, "outside" of the house.

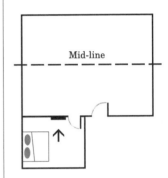

**Solutions:** The best that can be suggested for a master bedroom outside of the house is to position a mirror on the wall of the bedroom that would be closest to the house to symbolically reflect, or "draw," the room back into the main area of the home. Positioning of the mirror is important and might not work in all situations and in fact create a new problem if the mirror will be directly behind or in front of the bed. If the mirror can be covered by the head board or off to the side of the front of the bed, this solution will work quite well.

Some say it is alright to have a child's bedroom in an area of the house that extends out in front of the home, as children do come and go and will eventually be old enough to leave your house and begin a home of their own. Others say this leaves the child feeling unprotected, certainly unconnected, and likely to feel more comfortable and at home somewhere else. A home office is well suited to being in front of the house as the office is our business connection to the rest of the world. A kitchen in front of a home encourages meals to be eaten elsewhere or on the run.

### 123. Bedroom over a garage.

A bedroom situated over a garage is also experienced as disturbing to one's sleep. This should be especially avoided in apartment complexes built over a communal underground garage or street level car port with many cars constantly coming and going. As with other situations, some individuals are more sensitive to these influences than others and ultimately it will be your own experience that will determine if this is an unfortunate place to sleep. Worst of all is the electronic garage door opener usually positioned in the middle of the garage close to the ceiling.

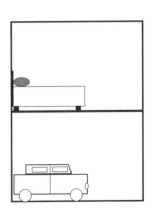

**Solutions:** One remedy that has been suggested is tacking a red ribbon from the ceiling of the garage to the floor of the garage and then tying a nine-inch red ribbon around the middle by making a bow. In this way you will have symbolically connected the bedroom with the earth below. Another variable of attaching a red ribbon from floor to ceiling is to paint a red line while another might be hanging a crystal on a red ribbon over each car in the garage to diffuse the negative ch'i. But remember the gaseous, toxic auto emissions will not be neutralized by crystals, ribbons or visualizations which may not be too much of a problem if the cars are rarely used.

The problem however will be increased if you live in an apartment over a communal garage with many cars going and coming and where tacking up ribbons and hanging crystals may not be feasible. If you do live over a communal garage, avoid apartments directly over the entrance into the garage and try and choose an apartment where there is the least amount of comings and goings. Tying the bed down with a rock hanging from the rope or having heavy items in the room may also help.

### 124. Inadequate space to walk on either side of the bed.

Often I am told that a prevailing health consideration is an inflamed hip or pelvis. Upon examining the bed placement in the bedroom, the reason becomes quite clear. Upon arising from the bed, there is not enough room to walk comfortably around to the front of the bed. The narrow squeeze necessitates a sideways "scooting" motion that puts extra pressure on one side of the body, compressing the hip joint, undermining that side's strength, and soon it buckles.

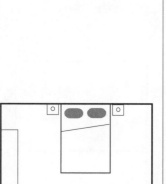

**Solutions:** Though the actual sprain may have happened at an aerobics class, playing tennis or dancing at a party, the underlying cause can usually be found in the home. If the bed is oversized for the room, get a smaller bed. If there is too much furniture for the size of the room, remove some of it. Sometimes it is easier just to move the bed a foot or two further from the wall to provide adequate space for the person sleeping on that side of the bed to be able to get up and walk comfortably.

### 125. Bedroom equality.

In addition to placement of the bed with a wall behind for support and a commanding view of the room and doorway, the bedroom should also be evaluated for satisfying other requirements to ensure calm restful sleep and relationship intimacy. One of these features is equality for both sides of the bed. This includes tables and lighting, space on both sides for equal ability to go to the master bath, or to leave the room.

Intimacy will also be diminished if the room is too vast or if the bed and furniture are oversized and it is difficult to move around. It is especially difficult if either partner has a narrow space to walk along to get to the front

of the bed, has to stumble over laundry, piles of books and magazines, or has to avoid bumping into sharp-pointed edges of furniture. Any or all of these difficulties make for great obstacles to overcome throughout the day and result in complaints, disparaging remarks, and overall unhappiness.

What each partner sees from their side of the bed is also of great importance. As mentioned above on page 108, #121, if one partner is looking into the bathroom while the other has a beautiful view out a window or is looking at a beautiful, up-lifting picture or arrangement, the conversation of each will reflect the view. One will be talking disapprovingly while focusing on the problems while the other will be talking about beauty and how wonderful life is. It doesn't take a rocket scientist to know which partner will be talking about what.

It is also very difficult to attract or keep a relationship if one side of the bed is totally up against a wall with no way for the person to easily get out. Climbing over the partner or scooting down to the end of the bed will work for a while but eventually the person who is "up against the wall" will want to live elsewhere. Bed situations like this usually represent a relationship that is falling apart or already has. More often then not, a bed up against the wall indicates a person who is sleeping alone as their partner seeks a more comfortable and compatable bedroom to have a relationship in – where they don't feel so constrained and where they "have room to move."

**Solutions:** Remember, in choosing a house, choosing the right bedroom is of great importance. So make sure you choose wisely. As stated, choose a bedroom that offers a solid wall behind the bed, no doorways to either side, adequate room to walk on either side, and one that provides a nice view or at least the space to hang uplifting images. Choose a bedroom that allows each side to enjoy equality.

## Double Happiness
*The stylized Chinese charater for "happiness" doubled.*

# Other Rooms to Consider

## Kitchen, Dining Room, Children's Room(s), Home Office, Garage

*Feng shui...is a method of helping ourselves and others
to live according to the Way of heaven
so that universal harmony will be preserved.*
~~ Eva Wong,
*Feng-Shui: The Ancient Wisdom of Harmonious Living for Modern Times*

• **Kitchen:** In some homes, the kitchen is the primary center of family activity: sharing meals, grabbing snacks, a place for the kids to do homework, late night conversations over a cup of tea, and one of the principal gathering places when entertaining guests.

## 126. Well-lit kitchen and with plenty of room or narrow and dark.

Narrow galley way kitchens tend to be less used and less inviting. Narrow kitchens tend to be good for boiling water for tea or coffee, grabbing a fast meal or a late night snack. A poorly lit kitchen is just uninviting. With doorway on either side they are "passage ways to somewhere else" and not a source of nourishment. Nor are narrow kitchens favorable for attracting or maintaining relationships and relationships that do exist will tend to be disturbed by bickering and discord. This is especially if the stove is opposite the sink or refrigerator (page 86, #120). A roomy, well-lit kitchen is nurturing to the body as well as to the soul.

> "If the cook is feeling vulnerable and tense the entire time they're cooking, when they bring the meal to the table, they might as well ask "How would you like your tension tonight?"
> ~~ Ralph & Lahni DeAmicis,
> *Feng Shui and the Tango in Twelve Easy Lessons*

**Solutions:** The best kitchen therefore is light and cheery, comfortable to move around and easy to keep clean. The best kitchens have adequate draws and cupboards and perhaps a walk-in pantry.

Attempts to enliven a kitchen might be done with a cheery, canary yellow paint, or flowery wallpaper, wall paper trim or ceramic tile. A kitchen can also be highlighted with a decorative floor mat in front of the sink and stove, a 40mm faceted lead-crystal sphere hanging from a nine-inch red ribbon, or if the ceiling is low, a three-inch red ribbon. Keep knives in drawers and avoid using the sink as dish, glass and silver storage.

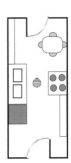

The smaller the kitchen the more important it is to brighten it with light color paint, pleasant decorations and to maintain it by keeping it clean and clutter free.

## 127. Cook in the Command Position.

As with the position of the bed in the bedroom or an office desk and chair

in the office, it is difficult to be relaxed and focused if you are forever anticipating that someone might be suddenly coming up behind you. In the kitchen
the cook needs to be able to see the door from wherever he or she is working.
This will be easy from some work stations while the proper placement of a
mirror will make this possible from other places.

**Solutions:** Some teachers suggest a large mirror over the stove to reflect the
abundance of food and to double your good fortune. Instead of "cooking on all
four," you can enjoy the metaphor of "cooking on all eight!" Be sure to use all
the burners and not neglect any as each burner represents good fortune
coming your way. Given that the position of the stove in many kitchens is up
against a wall, a mirror over the stove will give the cook the opportunity to
see if anyone is coming in from behind. Or, if the kitchen is large enough,
perhaps the stove can be repositioned to an island in the center of the kitchen
so the cook can see whomever is coming and going.

Remember, a happy cook cooks happy food which makes everyone happy,
and happy equals rested, nourished and healthy. Happy people go out into
the world and make happy money to bring back to keep the household happy.
"Happy" can also mean prosperous and harmonious. To enhance the area in
front of the stove, hang a small wind chime or 40mm faceted lead-glass
crystal prism to uplift the cook's energy.

### 128. Stove opposite sink, refrigerator or dishwasher.

In houses where the stove (Fire Ch'i) is opposite or next to a sink, refrigerator or dishwasher (Water Ch'i) arguments are likely as Fire and Water are
in conflict. If the kitchen is large enough, the arguing may be tempered but
in most kitchens with the Fire opposite the Water the arguments will be out
of control. Though an island stove may put the cook into the Command
Position, this is not so good if it is opposite the sink, refrigerator or dishwasher.

**Solutions:** One solution to try to restore harmony between the Fire and the
Water would be to hang a lead-glass crystal sphere midway between the two
Elements. The crystal can be at least 40mm and hung on a nine-inch red
ribbon or if the kitchen ceiling is too low a three-inch length of red ribbon
will do. In addition to the crystal prism, an area rug of an earthy color can be
placed on the floor to assist in separating the warring elements of Fire and
Water. If the Water Element is next to the Fire Element, a wood panel can be
put between the two as Water nourishes the Wood which will then feed the Fire.

### 129. Window behind the stove or stove next to the back or side door.

Positioning of the stove is also important. In olden days the stove was
kept hot by throwing logs into the fire. If a cold wind or even a warm breeze
blew into the mouth of the stove, the fire would be cooled and possibly put

out. The meal could possibly be ruined. Even today in this modern world, the emotional identification of the stove as a source of nourishment will effect our everyday activities if something isn't quite right.

Though it is unlikely that anyone except for a few people living quite remote use wood burning stoves, the vast majority of people in modern times use gas or electric (page 132, #155 – Get rid of the microwave), and a breeze blowing can affect the proper cooking of the food. The real problem however is that the subconscious interprets the wind blowing over the stove as blowing prosperity away.

**Solutions:** As the stove is a symbol of prosperity, it should be kept clean with all burners working properly and it should be situated in a safe, secure area of the kitchen.

### 130. Bathroom directly above the stove.

Another example of the awareness in the subconscious of waste and other bathroom activity going on above the important prosperity symbol, the stove.

**Solutions:** Often there are cupboards above the stove enabling you to put a mirror on top of the cabinet to deflect the second floor bathroom energy away from the stove. If there is no cupboard, consider taping a small oval mirror to the ceiling directly above the stove with the mirrored surface facing upward.

• **Dining Room:** A dining room table in chaos, or any area of the home that is chaotic, indicates life styles that are frenetic with the constant feeling of being overwhelmed by all that needs to be done and all that hasn't yet been done.

### 131. Dining room table positioned between two doors.

Ch'i flows rapidly between two open doors opposite each other making it uncomfortable to sit at a table situated between two doors. Such a situation is not conducive for the family sitting together. Dining room tables located between two doorways tend to be used only on special occasions or formal occasions. Whether every day family meals or formal occasions, family members or guests will leave the room soon after the meal is finished or sit and squirm until permission is given. When not being used for meals, dining room tables between two doors are often used as a catch-all for whatever is coming in or going out of the house (mail, groceries, library books, etc.) and for incomplete projects in progress as the large table is a great place to pile stuff.

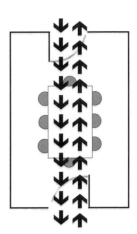

**Solutions:** Unless at least one of the dining room doors can be kept close, all you can do is make a concerted attempt to resist the temptation to let chaos take over the dining room table, the symbol of nourishment and civility.

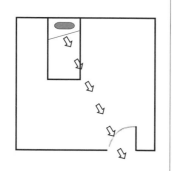

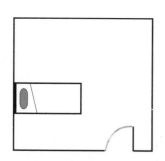

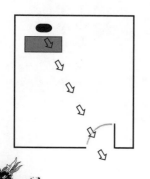

• **Children's Room(s):** It is not uncommon for parents to rent or buy a home without considering the feng shui needs of their children. They see the child's room as a space "they will get used to." And yes, just like any growing "thing," they will learn to compromise and compensate in order to survive. If we want children to develop in a truly healthy manner, both emotionally and physically, we have to provide them with not just the best educational opportunities, but also the best bedroom feng shui as possible so that they develop balanced personalities and a strong individuality.

### 132. Child's bed in the Command Position (page 100, #111 – Beds in the Command Position).

Children are usually tired from a full day of activity that they seem to sleep anywhere. But they sleep better if their bed is in the Command Position of the room where they can see the entrance of the room but are not in direct alignment of either the entrance (page 100, #112 – Coffin Position), a bathroom door or other door in front of, behind or along side of the bed. Beds in any of these unfortunate positions will result in the child getting frequent colds, alergies, or other maladies.

### 133. Child's bed with the headboard against a solid wall with space for ch'i to flow around the front and on both sides.

It is not uncommon to find the child's bed pushed up against a wall in order to maximize the play space in the center of the room. Though play space is beneficial, a bed against the wall stunts the development of the child. Like a plant on a table near a window, growth becomes one-sided until you turn the plant and allow other side to receive the energizing rays of the sun.

Until 6 to 7 years of age, a child can benefit from the womb-like protection of a partially enclosed sleeping space. But as a child "expands" into the world, self-worth and the ability to "reach out" to others needs to be encouraged. If the left side of the bed is up against the wall, the child's self-worth and self-confidence will become an issue. If it is the right side of the body that is up against a wall, the child's ability to reach out to others will be inhibited.

**Solutions:** Having a bed with the headboard against a solid wall is as ideal for a child as it is for adults and is to be preferred. If the room is too small for this arrangement, at least move the bed two to three inches from the wall to allow the ch'i to flow on both sides and still be able to enjoy the benefits of maximum play space in the center of the room.

### 134. Child's desk in the Command Position.

Children are easily distracted and even more so if their desk is against the wall with their back to the entrance to the room. Once again this arrangement is often a convenient attempt to maximize play space in the center of the room. Fact is, a child who can't see the door from his desk will rarely sit at the bedroom desk curious to know what's going on elsewhere. Instead the child will do homework at the kitchen table in an attempt to feel part of the family activity.

**Solutions:** Turn the desk around so the child can see the door and will feel he or she "knows" what's going on in the main part of the house. In this way the child will not feel excluded. Of course teenagers often want to close the door to their room so they can feel they have privacy and feel secure no one is watching them as they do teenager things. But even for teenagers with a desk up against a wall with their back to the door, there will still be a nervous insecurity. As for an adult in a similar situation, if the desk can not be turned around, the simple cure is to mount a mirror on the desk or wall, or a mirror adapted to sitting on top of the computer monitor.

### 135. Large windows in the children's room.

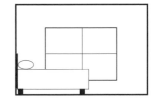

Windows and doorways can have different associations. In some cases, a doorway is like a "mouth" with the front door being the "mouth of ch'i." Windows are like the "eyes" of the house. Another association is that doorways are the "voice of the adults" living in the home while the windows of the house represent the "voice of the children." Large windows in a child's room consequently can be a problem as large windows stimulate the child to speak with a "loud voice."

**Solutions:** If remodeling is possible, this would be best. But at least curtains can be hung on these windows to scale them down to a manageable size. Pull-up shades can also help regulate the over stimulating ch'i flow from large windows.

### 136. Beam over a child's bed or desk area (page 106, #118 – Beam over the bed).

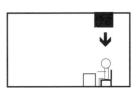

Children are no different than adults when it comes to feeling uncomfortable and insecure sitting or sleeping under a weight-bearing beam. All through the night the child will wiggle and squirm in an attempt to get out from under it. The compressed ch'i beneath the beam often results in illness or an accident.

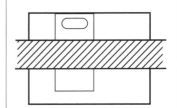

**Solutions:** Cover all beams directly over the bed with fabric or finish the whole ceiling with drywall or plywood. Roof supports can sometimes be painted with faux finishes or cloud like patterns to blend the roof supports into the ceiling and thereby lift it up. Otherwise hang two bamboo flutes and other decorative objects on the beam to alter its unnatural straightness and create a meandering pattern. Children art is often the perfect solution for many feng shui problems.

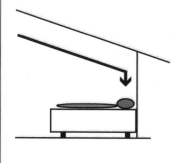

### 137. Sloped-ceiling over a child's bed or desk area (page 107, #119).

As with a beam over a bed, a sloped-ceiling can be disorientating as the mind feels most comfortable with symmetry and a sloped-ceiling forces the brain to compensate in an attempt to maintain balance.

Sloped-ceilings can be especially difficult if the child's room is a converted attic or crawl space with a peaked roof with a radical incline and very little wall space between it and the floor of the upstairs room. At first this may seem fun, like a hideout, especially when the child is young and shorter in stature than when a teenager and significantly beginning to grow out of this awkwardly shaped space.

**Solutions:** As with the overall philosophy of feng shui which states that a home is a container that shapes the inhabitants, so an irregularly shaped room whether distorted by a strange angular walls or a pitched roof will equate to strange mental and emotional development.

### 138. Child's room upstairs and the parent's room down stairs, or child's room toward the back of the house and the parent's room toward the front.

As with a house uphill from another (page 59, #47 and page 60, #48), or even with bunk beds, the one on top will try to "lord" it over those below. Children who live upstairs and the parents down, or children in the back and the parents toward the front of a home, are children who assume control of the household affairs as they relate to the child's needs, expectations, and perhaps, demands.

**Solutions:** As with page 59, #47 – House uphill from another on the same property, it is important for the property owners to retain authority over their property. So too in a family, it is important for the parents to maintain parental authority over the children. The same remedy can be applied using a photo of the parents. Put a picture of the parents in the furthest corner of either the up or down stairs depending on where the child is and thereby symbolically take back the control of the household. And continually remind the child(ren) to say "please" and "thank you" and never treat the parents like servants.

### 139. Each child has their own space.

If there are more than two children, they each need to have their own space with a place to keep their clothes, their special toys, and an individual bed.

Bunk beds are another attempt to maximize a child's play space to the psychological detriment of the children involved. As with one house being uphill from another, the residents of the uphill home will tend to "lord it over" those lower down the hill. The human inclination to establish a pecking order seems ingrained in the human social psyche. Bunk beds seem to reinforce this inclination with the child on the upper level dominating the child on the lower level.

Another thing that continually surprises me about homes with bunk beds is how infrequently either parent takes the time to get in the lower bunk bed to assess the situation. Often when I get into the lower bunk bed to check the feng shui, I look up and see the under side of the upper bunk bed with springs, wires and mattress markings.

**Solutions:** If you have no alternative to using bunk beds, at least decorate the underside for your child or help them decorate as they want. Help them create a pleasant sleep environment by avoiding over-stimulating colors and images of action figures, circus scenes or any other imagery that is anything but restful. The theme should be calm, peaceful and dreamy.

There are not too many solutions for establishing equality between the two children. If bunk beds is the only arrangement possible, perhaps the child with the more dominant personality can be put in the lower level in order to give the child with a milder disposition a slight advantage.

**•Home Office:** As more and more individuals work from their home, the status of the home office from a feng shui perspective is becoming increasingly important. By home office we do not mean a desk that is used occasionally for checking E-mail or writing checks and stamping envelopes. But rather an integral part of an individual's everyday labors that bring personal income in to use in fulfilling the family's needs.

## 140. Home office large enough.

Home offices are frequently stuck in the corner of a kitchen, a hallway between rooms, or wherever else adequate space can be carved out. This may be adequate for answering family correspondence, signing checks to pay bills and arranging the child's after school activities but a claustrophobic small room with no room to move (breathe) or situated in a distracting thoroughfare of household activity, is unlikely to be an office reflecting financial and creative success.

**Solution:** If you are expecting to earn a decent living and enjoying the work you have chosen to do, choose a home with a room that can be set aside to be the office. If the work you do is dependent on your contacts with the outside world, a front room is best as a back room encourages reclusiveness.

If the room is small, avoid the temptation to build upwards as high shelves with books or supplies on the uppermost shelves will be worried about – "what if they fall" – so keep the office shelving to no higher than your head when you are seated. It is also important to avoid surrounding yourself

to closely with sources of electro-magnetic radiation. Keep as many electrical devices as possible elsewhere in the room and consider wearing an electro-magnetic neutralizer such as the Crystal Catalyst® which will neutralize whatever electro-magnetic radiation you are exposed to. (See last page for ordering information.)

### 141. Quiet and an uplifting view from the home office window.

As with the view from bedroom windows, what you see is what inspires you. A room with a view is especially important as disturbing views of city chaos or country views of a stagnant pond will soon sour an otherwise creative mind. A room off the main thoroughfare that is quiet will be more conducive to work well done than being bombarded by abrasive automotive or industrial noise.

**Solutions:** If your home office plays a significant part in the daily activity of earning an income, working on income producing projects and where thought and contemplation are necessary for setting goals and evaluating progress then choose a place of business or a home office location with a clear view. Definitely do not choose a spot with "poison arrows" shooting at you from neighboring roof lines or pathways and roadways.

If it is not possible to find an office with a view, career success can still be strengthened by hanging a picture opposite your desk that allows you to feel uplifted when you look up. Perhaps it could be a picture that stimulates creativity and the willingness to take a chance. Be careful not to hang a picture of lofty mountain peaks as the subconscious will continually be challenged to "climb" that mountain. Use only landscape or waterscape pictures that are calm and inspirational. Or a map of the world? Or how about a boat coming to port laden with cargo and other treasures?

### 142. Office desk in the Command Position.

In evaluating the placement of the bed, desks or the dining room table the Command Position is always the best. The Command Position is a variation of the Arm Chair as described as the best siting for a home.

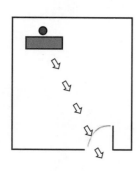

Imagine sitting on a chair that had no arm rests or backing. You would certainly feel unstable fighting the tendency to fall over backwards. This precarious feeling will result in nervous anxiety and a resultant loss of focus and concentration. Put the backing and arms back on the arm chair and the feeling is one of empowerment, of being solidly in the driver's seat.

If the desk cannot be positioned to see the doorway into the room, there will be great discomfort as one constantly wonders what is going on behind his back. This will have terrible consequences at work as much indeed will be going on behind the back such as back-stabbing, embezzleing, malingering, gossip, etc.

**Solution:** Position the arm chair with a wall behind it for support and on the wall hang a picture of a mountain or any positive uplifting image so your sense of security and being on purpose will be further reinforced.

### 143. Office desk with a window behind it.

A window behind an office chair such as the President of the United States has in the Oval Office, weakens the focus and removes the sense of support. Of course in earthquake, hurricane, or tornado areas of the country this threatening reality will enhance the distracting anxiety and constant feelings of vulnerability.

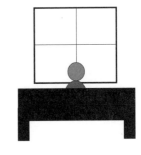

**Solution:** A fellow feng shui practitioner informed me of a photograph of former President John F. Kennedy in the White House Oval Office showing an elephant sculpture on the window sill behind the desk. An elephant would be symbolic of a "small mountain" thereby giving Kennedy support and in fact he is likely to have been the most supported president (though like all presidents had his scandalous shortcomings which were not made known until long after his assassination). Indeed, any individual with a window behind his desk will feel as though he is "falling over backwards." Placing a small elephant symbolizing a small mountain on the window sill may help considerably. A short decorative screen will also give the feeling of being supported especially if there is an image such as a mountain to reinforce this feeling of support.

### 144. Toilet in direct line with the office desk and chair.

The toilet itself "radiates" negative ch'i both forward and back. Looking at a floor plan should make it quite clear if the front or back of the toilet is in direct line with where a desk will be positioned. The negative toilet energy is mostly associated with ill-health (page 103, #114 – Toilet in direct line with the bed). The effect negative toilet ch'i has on an office desk and chair is an undermining of business prosperity and opportunity. Do not underestimate this problem.

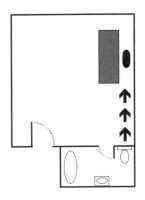

**Solution:** Whether the bathroom is connected to the home office or situated elsewhere in the house, the desk and chair should be shielded from the toilet by placing at least a 24" x 30 - 36" mirror behind or in front of the toilet to reflect the toilet energy back onto itself. The mirror can be positioned in the bathroom itself or on the other side of the wall from the toilet in the adjoining room. If the mirror is placed behind the tank, it can be camouflaged by putting wood or cloth on the tank and a decorative object on top. If the mirror is being place in the adjoining room, it can be placed behind a piece of furniture or in a closet but be sure to place with the mirrored-side facing the front or back of the toilet.

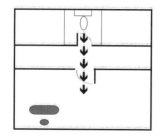

### 145. Bathroom door opposite the office door.

Just another variation of the negative bathroom energetic leading your thoughts and your success "down the drain" or getting "flushed down" the toilet. What you see when you leave your office has a strong effect on the subconscious. And bathrooms and toilets are synonymous with waste, flushing and the opposite of where you want your thoughts to be.

**Solution:** If you get stuck with a bathroom door opposite your office door or any other frequently used door of the house, affix a mirror to the outside of the door to "bounce" the auspicious ch'i away. If you hang a mirror, be sure to hang it securely so it doesn't generate a need to worry about "what if the mirror breaks" if the door is closed too hard.

Frameless mirrors can be hung with mirror hangers in all corners. A framed mirror can be hung on a wire but then earthquake putty (sold at most hardware stores) can be pressed on each of the lower corners to secure it tightly. Other decorations can be considered such as framed-pictures with landscapes or other scenes that give a sense of depth while the glass over the picture reflects the good ch'i away.

• **Garage:** If the garage is a separate structure, how the garage is utilized is less important than when it is attached to the main house. In most modern homes not only is the garage attached but there is a door connecting the garage with the rest of the house – sometimes through a utility room and sometimes directly into an important room such as the kitchen.

### 146. Garage large enough for cars, storage or other uses.

It is quite common for a home owning family to have at least two cars and in need of extra storage or living space. Choices have to be made. Turn it into a family room, extra bedroom, or keep it for cars and storage? Garages are sometimes the only place to locate the washer-dryer and extra refrigerator. Garages are busy places.

**Solution:** With growing families garages often get chaotically overloaded as they try to serve multi-purposes. If the garage is also needed for exercise equipment, workshop or teenage drum rehearsal space, consider a three car garage.

Social conditioning seems to dictate that the garage is under the rulership of the man of the house just as the kitchen is most typically the domain of the wife. Be that as it may, whoever holds sway over the garage, needs to keep it organized as the garage is a place of transition between the outside world and the world of the home. Storage closets are best but if you use open shelves consider installing curtains that can be closed to cover the chaotic appearance of the various household items that are likely to be stored in the garage.

*Section III*

# Additional Feng Shui Secrets
# Ancient & Modern

## Understanding Your Self

Knowing ourselves
leads to understanding the world
around us, and in turn, knowledge of the world leads
to greater understanding of the self.
At a very deep level,
the Feng Shui of an environment
has the power to support our search
for self-realization and outward expression.
Surrounded by harmony, we are aided in achieving balance
for ourselves and for those whose lives we touch.
When we look up at the clouds,
or feel the soil between our fingers,
we are ultimately examining our own souls.

~~ Dr. Baolin Wu and Jessica Eckstein,
*Lighting the Eye of the Dragon: Inner Secrets of Taoist Feng Shui*

Double Happiness

# Wealth and Partnership Areas of the Home

## The Ba-gua Template

*Remember: Your home mirrors your life and the energy patterns
that you send out to the world. Try to decode the messages
that your energy is sending out, for hidden in those signals
is another aspect of who you are,
waiting to be embraced, acknowledged, and transformed.*
~~Nancy SantoPietro, *Feng Shui: Harmony By Design*

The square or rectangle are two shapes that represent stability in a world of uncertainty. When we come home to our home, we want to feel safe and secure so we can rest, raise a family, and enjoy certain pleasures of life such as eating, lovemaking, and so forth. The square or rectangle most appropriately symbolizes that dependable reality. All other shapes, therefore, lacking in that solid four-square-wall symmetry, lacks dependability. Too many angles "shoot" harmful sha ch'i into too many directions. Odd shapes generate dysfunctional thoughts and behavior. Some individuals are more vulnerable than others and will display the effect of odd shapes quicker but all people will eventually be affected.

## Ba-Gua Template

In the first section of these feng shui guidelines for evaluating a home you are buying, renting or currently living in, we examined primarily environmental influences on what we can call the "external and internal landscape" of the house. We analyzed how the ch'i flowing in and around the home may affect our lives and how some ch'i can directly affect us physically (ex: high mountain tops, relationship of doorways to the bed, etc.) and some indirectly affecting us physically by disturbing our subconscious symbolically (ex: "hidden arrows," spiral staircase, beams, etc.). Another important way we see how our environment influences our lives is based on how we subconsciously assign different areas of the house to represent different areas of our life which in feng shui are called: the Eight Aspirations.

There is more than one way to project this alignment. One method is to assign each Aspiration to one of the eight directions of the compass. In this system Southeast is the Wealth Area and the Southwest is the Partnership Area. If this is the system you already know, continue to use it. If this concept is new to you, or you have already studied the Ba-gua orientated to the wall the front door is on, then the Wealth Area is the far left corner from

the door into the house or room and the Partnership Areas is the far right corner of the house or room. Both systems work very well and like all systems of feng shui sometimes they clash but usually they blend easily.

Regardless of which system you prefer, using the Armchair metaphor discussed early in the book, the back of the house or property is regarded as stronger than the more vulnerable front. The left side of the house is also seen as different than the right side. The left side is seen as a projection of our more aggressive left side of our brain while the right side of the home reflects the more intimate and sensitive right side of the brain. Using this typography we project our "stronghold" for abundance to the safer back left side of the home rather than position it near the front door. Likewise, the back far right side will correspond to the Partnership Area of our subconscious. In this manner each Aspiration falls into a different area of the house as described in the Ba-gua Template (see illustations below). The Eight Aspirations are: Abundance, Fame, Partnership, Creativity/Children, Benefactors/Helpful People, Career, Knowledge/Academics, and Family.

The eight-sided Ba-gua Template ("ba" means eight, "gua" means side) is traditionally inscribed with one of the Eight Trigrams or combinations of three lines, either broken or solid, referred to in Chinese as yin-lines and yang-lines. It is the combination of these three lines of yin and yang that gives rise to the different Aspirations much in the same fashion as modern day computers use on and off switches in their circuitry boards. In short, the Trigrams utilize the same Binary Code as modern computer programming which is a series of on/off switches which allow the information (ch'i) in any given computer program to flow and be utilized.

### THREE DOOR BA-GUA

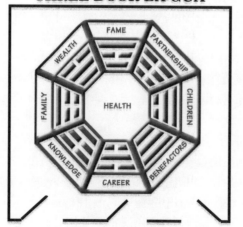

The entry way into the house, room or onto the property determines the location of each of the Eight Aspirations.

### COMPASS SCHOOL BA-GUA

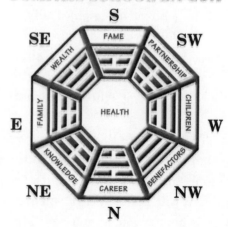

The meaning of the Eight Trigrams determines the compass directions and the location of each of each of the Eight Aspirations.

The above is a brief introduction to a complicated subject and in many ways is an over simplification which you can further research in other books mentioned in the Bibliography. For our purposes let us move on to what problems to avoid in choosing a home you may want to purchase or rent.

## 147. Hill sloping down behind the house weakens the Ba-gua Template.

Where the eye goes, so goes one's thoughts and consequently one's ch'i. As mentioned above, the ideal house site is strengthened by a hill behind the dwelling creating the Armchair effect. Obversely, a hill sloping down and away from the house is the equivalent of removing the backing of an arm chair and then constantly making adjustments not to fall over backwards. Or, if there is no protection from behind, then you'll always feel uncomfortably exposed and insecure as you nervously have to watch your back.

Whichever rationalization you choose to follow adds up to about the same, either one or all three of the Aspirations of Wealth, Fame or Partnership will literally "go down hill" as you struggle to keep it together. Though there are suggested cures for this sort of a situation, the best cure is to not rent or buy a house with a hill sloping behind it. Especially if this negative factor is further reinforced by a roadway, a back door or a bathroom in the Wealth or Partnership Area, etc.

**Solution:** To offset the weakening of the Ba-gua by the down hill slope, the proper use of colors (gold, red, purple for Wealth; pink, white, pastels for Partnerships) and symbols will do much to strengthen these Aspirations. In addition a flag on a pole at the bottom of the slope will help "lift" the ch'i back up. Even stronger might be a flood light on a pole at the bottom of the slope hot-wired to the house, pointing to the roof to "shoot" the energy back to the house whenever it is turned on. The light bulb need only be turned on once to activate its intention.

Recently I was called in to walk four acres located on the side of a mountain. Beautiful topography. Gentle sloping allowed for a few excellent house sites featuring unobstructed ocean views. The one chosen by the landowners was overlooking a gulch. Very magical with fern covered slopes, tall gnarly trunk *robusta eucalyptus* trees, and a deep marriage of mystery and nature's wild place. The devic energy was quite strong.

I immediately suggested they move the house away from the cliff about a hundred yards so the side and not the back of the house was facing the gulch. With a gulch behind the home, the Abundance, Fame and Partnership Areas would have nothing to support them. Money, reputation and relationships could all go downhill, or down the gulch. These would be problematic enough to result in the residents becoming "edgy" from "living on the edge." "Edgy" equals nervous, jittery and short-tempered. It is difficult to feel calm, focused and secure when you are living on the edge. People living on the edge literally become "edgy."

Not only does an upward-sloping hill behind the house provide support to these three Guas but by putting a large deck on the side of the home facing the gulch, it allows the residents to visit the devas in their wild place rather than bring the wild place into the home.

### 148. Missing Corners.

A missing corner is determined by measuring each side of the structure and discovering that one side extends at least half way the length of the whole house but not all the way. The corner that is notched out of the square or rectangular-shape is referred to as a missing corner.

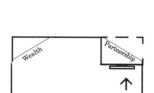

A back corner of the home will symbolize Abundance to the far left (or SE) and Partnership to the far right (or SW). These Aspirations can be further undermined if the property slopes downward or has a road or river flowing by. In other words be careful in your evaluation that you can more than adequately compensate for a missing back corner of the house. Front corners can also be troublesome but are usually easier to compensate for. As the Ba-gua Template can be mapped out on each room of the house, each room also has a Wealth and Partnership Area, making possible to stimulate these corners to overcome the negative implications of a home with a missing corner.

**Solution:** In many cases this can be remedied by filling in the missing corner with a patio, landscaping, or an outside features such as a birdbath or sculpture. But in many other cases the consequence of a missing corner can be disastrous especially if it is difficult to implement an outside patio, landscaping, etc.

Mirrors can also be installed on the inside wall to give the illusion of depth and that the room extends into the missing area. Consider too that as you remedy the inside wall for the feeling of irregularity, you can also energize the two corners that have resulted from one corner being absent. In this sense you now have two Abundance Areas or two Partnership Areas.

The presence of a structural support in any of the corners may also indicate that there are problems in that area of life as the aggressive edge "cuts" into that area of consciousness. For example: an exposed structural support in the Partnership Area of the home can represent relationship problems.

### 149. An overly large extension in any of the areas of the house.

An extension is determined by measuring the outside wall of a home from corner to corner. If one side extends pass the outer wall but is less than 50% than it is termed and extension. (A missing corner is more than 50% – see above #148).

A slight extension is considered favorable as it will be stimulating to the area of the Ba-gua that has the extension. For example: in the Wealth Area, it means greater prosperity.

However, if the extension is overly large, it can be overly expansive

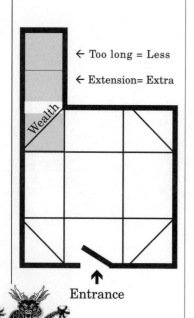

← Too long = Less

← Extension= Extra

Entrance

bringing negative consequences. In the Fame Area it can give false expectations or an inflated sense of self-importance. In the Wealth Area it can bring over self-confidence in gambling or investing. In the Benefactors Area, it could represent being constantly let down by those who offer assistance. In the Partnership Area it could represent lack of intimacy and confused affinities.

**Solution:** To mitigate these adverse circumstances strengthen these Aspirations in other rooms of the home. In the room that is over expanded try to decorate to create more focus and sense of proportion.

## 150. Bathroom in the Wealth, Health or Partnership Areas.

Just as missing corners are not desirable so too having your bathroom in any of the corners will present a challenge. The areas to not even consider having to deal with would be having your bathroom in your Wealth or Partnership Areas as you do not want to have either "go down the toilet," "down the drain," or "washed out" by the excessive water of the bathroom. As with a bathroom in any of the corners, appropriate colors and symbols (see Solutions, #147 above) can be used to strengthen the Aspiration associated with these corners to overcome the good ch'i being drained by the bathroom.

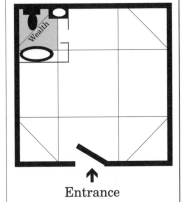

Entrance

**Solutions:** Quite frankly there are some teachers who say nothing will work. I do not feel this is totally true nor am I totally convinced that all situations are workable to a point.

To overcome the draining influence at least keep the toilet seat down and the bathroom door closed. This is a good practice regardless of where the toilet is located. In fact, consider hanging a mirror on the outside of the door to deflect good ch'i from entering the bathroom. This is especially recommended if the bathroom is in the Wealth Corner of the home.

Also consider hanging a 40mm lead-glass crystal prism sphere to diffuse the ch'i that does enter the bathroom. The sphere should be hung between the door into the bathroom and the toilet. It has been suggested that the sphere be hung on a nine-inch red ribbon (embroidery floss or silk cord). If the the ceiling is low, three-inches will suffice (three is a multiply of nine – all odd numbers are strong yang number – nine being the strongest).

For the Partnership Area the colors should be soft and intimate such as pink, pastels or even white. Yellow, an earth color, can be used to absorb the water. Avoid watery-colors (most blues, dark colors and many greens) that will add to the dampness.

For the Wealth Area recommended colors are warm colors but avoid gold as you do not want to "flush" your wealth away. Nor have any pictures of family members so you don't "flush" their wealth away either. In the Partner-

ship Area you can have images of couples whether two Mandarin ducks or two people walking holding hands along a pleasant pathway. But the best solution is to find a home that does not have a bathroom in either Wealth or Partnership Areas and I hope you do not choose such a home.

### 151. Back doors or large windows in the Wealth or Partnership Areas of the home.

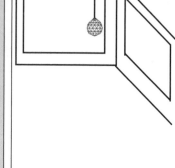

The home like a container needs walls, windows and doors to hold onto whatever ch'i flows in. Psychologically, the corners are needed for strong structural support. Ch'i accumulates in corners. When the corners are two windows coming together at a right angle, ch'i "leaks out" and a sense of fragility is projected. With a "weak" far left back corner (or SE), wealth is lost, with a "weak" far right back corner (or SW), relationships are strained. This weakness is also found in homes with back doors in either rear corner.

**Solution:** If there are two windows, a curtain can be hung in the corner to make a solid corner that can "hold" ch'i. Perhaps a small table can be placed there with appropriate symbols of wealth or relationship according to which corner is being strengthened. A 40mm lead-glass crystal sphere can be hung on a nine-inch red ribbon as an additional energizer. If it is a back door "leaking" energy, beside keeping the door close and curtained if it is partial glass or sliding glass doors, hang a wind chime outside the door and place symbolic items in the actual corners as stabilizers.

### 152. Mother-in-law's or children's room in Partnership Area.

Ideally, the master bedroom should be in the Partnership Area of the Ba-Gua Template. Any room that is used by both partners or the family would also be acceptable such as a kitchen, dining room or even an office. However, a child (especially a step-child), a mother-in-law, or any relative or friend in the Partnership Area will dominate the primary relationship of the household either by distracting the couple with their pre-occupations and demands or causing conflict in one form or another.

**Solutions:** It is beneficial to place a photograph of the home's primary relationship in the Partnership Area to strengthen the relationship and to put such a picture in the corner of the room in the Partnership Area of the home. If an actual photograph seems out of place, as may be indicated by a step-child or room mate, then something representing the couple – perhaps a gift or some item symbolic of the couple's intimacy and love – may be hung or placed on the window sill. But placing a photograph or symbolic object should be done like all remedies with very strong intention in order for it to be most effective.

# Things to Change If You Can
## Contributors to Poor Feng Shui

*Feng Shui is based on the premise that people experience happier, healthier,
more prosperous lives when their home and work environments
are harmonious. As with human bodies, the "healthier" the bodies
of our buildings are, the more they support us in living a rich,
creative and joyful existence.*
~~ Terah Kathryn Collins,
*The Western Guide to Feng Shui*

Many problems that we encounter in examining the home cannot be changed without considering extensive and sometimes expensive remodeling. Remodeling, as we have seen, may be the best solution for removing decorative pillars that obstruct ch'i flow that hopefully are not providing crucial weight-bearing support for the roof or upper floors. Some homes come with features that are easily removed. If an apartment or house is rented, you might be able to get approval from the owner of the building to remove items or features you do not like or wish to live with. In some cases things can be put carefully in storage and then replaced when you move.

### 153. Ceiling fans.

Ceiling fans, though better than air conditioning in regard to the air you breathe, still emanate an electro-magnetic field from their AC/DC motors. Apart from this factor, the main problem is the "chopping" motion of the blades. The whirling blades overhead generates fear and uncertainty as the chop, chop, chop movement is felt as a threat to the subconscious which fears these rotating blades as potentially "flying off" and hitting you. Ceiling fans directly above the head disturbs the heart and nervous system as they "grind" away.

Ceiling fans that are acceptable are high above or at least not directly above sitting areas where they "chop" the aura and crown chakra or over sleeping areas where they "chop" the legs and feet. Some ceiling fans have attached light fixtures which further add to the visual clutter especially if you have to duck to avoid hitting your head when walking by. Ceiling fans which wobble on their stems are of course the least desirable. It probably will not fly off and hit anyone. Even though it is securely bolted to a ceiling rafter, the "what if it flies free" screams loudly to the subconscious to get out of harm's way.

Ceiling fans are relatively easy to remove and can be replaced with a low profile ceiling light fixture. A suitable substitute for the cooling aspect of the

*Hang a small
lead-glass crystal
prism from pull
cord of over head
fan to deflect
chopping action
of blades.*

overhead fan are floor fans such as those made by Vornado. These deep scoop fans are designed to circulate the air similar to an air conditioner. They are also easily put away and out of sight when not needed and easily taken out when they are unlike ceiling fans which remain unused dust collectors for most of the year. If you can not remove the ceiling fan then diffuse the "chopping" by hanging a 40mm lead-glass crystal sphere from the pull cord.

## 154. Remove louvered windows and vertical blinds.

Remove louvered windows and vertical blinds as these straight edges emanate "hidden arrows" as they "slice" the interior space when partially opened. If there is no way to replace them consider keeping them completely closed or completely opened so the cutting edges are not "cutting" you and your fellow occupants. If they can not be removed, as much as possible keep louvered windows and vertical blinds covered with curtains.

## 155. Electric stove or gas – get rid of the microwave.

Wood fires are the most energizing method of cooking food and the most impractical in modern dwellings. This makes gas cooking the best and most acceptable. Electric stoves are good enough if you have no choice but they do not radiate the food like wood or gas.

Microwaves are not even to be considered as a means of cooking food. In fact they do not cook food but rather rearrange the molecules. Radiant heat from wood or gas "energizes" food cooked by these means making it yang, strong, and vitalized. Food prepared by a microwave remains yin, weak, and devitalized as the food never becomes energized. Microwave ovens also have the negative effect of fixing protein molecules making them impossible to digest. Furthermore, the outside is not as hot as the inside of the item microwaved which deceives the palate to eat and swallow which can overheat the stomach lining. Over a period of time these various shocks to the body put the body into a pre-cancerous condition.

## 156. Fluorescent light fixtures.

Fluorescent light fixtures are another bane of modern design that can be held accountable for aggravating the psyche of many individuals especially in office buildings and other work places. Fluorescent lights present two problems: one, they flicker and hum incessantly and two, they usually lack the full spectrum of colors found in natural light. Being top heavy in yellow and the active colors, they over stimulate the nervous system – "frying" the nervous system may be a more apt description.

Needless to say, in bedrooms, kitchens or anywhere in the home that is frequently used, fluorescent lights with the continuous humming and flicker-

ing of the ballast with or without purple in the light output results in individuals experiencing recurrent headaches, nervous irritability, shortened attention span, depression and anti-social behavior.

Full spectrum bulbs are available in many hardware, health food and lighting fixture stores. Even better is to remove these monsters of electronics and replace them with full spectrum soft lighting provided by incandescent. Ott lights are better and can also be obtained at most lighting fixture stores and are offered in many mail order catalogues.

### 157. Stairs without risers – "floating stairs."

Stairs without risers which are usually found outside a dwelling as part of a porch or taking you to a second floor landing are sometimes found inside a home as well. This stairway construction is incomplete and allows the ch'i to "slip through the cracks" so to speak. The usual solution is to put a backing on these steps, install a runner carpet with a "meandering" design that flows from step-to-step or, if possible, to place some potted plants underneath to catch the ch'i and bring it back.

### 158. Thorny bushes or pointy-leaf plants.

Thorny bushes or pointy-leaf plants along pathways should be removed or at least trimmed back as pointy-leaf plants are considered aggressive and hostile. Likewise, pointy-leaf plants near seating areas inside or outside of the house are perceived as uncomfortable and under most circumstances people will not sit near them. In similar manner, people do not feel comfortable walking along a path with thorny roses, bougainvillea or cactus reaching out to scratch their skin or tear at their clothing.

### *Peonies*
*Symbol of harmonious love relationship.*
**Chinese paper cutting folk art.**

# Things to Fix Immediately

## Keeping the Home in Good Condition

Have nothing in your home
that you do not know to be useful
or believe to be beautiful.
~~ William Morris, artist & designer

Maintenance is of great importance in feng shui theory as anything that is not right becomes a disturbance to one's equanimity and distracting to one's focus. Any tension becomes undermining to one's well-being and upsetting to relationship harmony which in turn distracts from one's ability to be creative and productive inevitably affecting one's prosperity. All of these life situations will continue to spiral out of control if there are additional life upheavals with the more intense disturbances resulting in the greatest upsets requiring the most effort to overcome in order to reestablish balance and equanimity.

I often think of the analogy of rolling a tire across an empty room. In all likelihood the tire will hit the wall on the opposite side of the room. However, if there is one pencil on the floor in the tires path, that tire will either roll over it or be slowed down by it depending on the size and speed of the tire. If there are many small items in the tire's path, the tire has that many more obstacles to overcome. Again, depending on the size and speed of the tire, the tire will either overcome the obstacles or be knocked off course.

In a similar manner, if we wake up in the morning and have to confront a blank wall and then step over books and clutter around the bed and squeeze by a sharp-pointed dresser and a towering armoire, by the time we get through the bathroom routine, get dressed, and are ready for breakfast, the psychological toll is heavy – our psyche is already grumbling and perhaps not silently.

If this is indicative of the pattern of the day, going to work on a crowded freeway and sitting in an office or place of business with equally as difficult feng shui, the breaking point is soon reached. Something has got to give and it is always the weakest link either emotional or physical. It is with this in mind that taking action to keep one's environment stress-free and harmonious is of the greatest importance. Use feng shui to identify and solve major problems but don't neglect to keep the basic maintanence in good order. Therefore, fixing that which needs fixing or adjusting feng shui cures that need adjusting, helps to

maintain one's highest intention and continues to attract beneficial circumstances.

### 159. Leaky plumbing.

Leaky plumbing or dripping faucets are usually the first thing mentioned in magazine articles introducing feng shui to the public. Money, also called "currency," flows like water and leaky plumbing and dripping faucets are immediately experienced as loss of income or income coming in and "leaking" away. No water becomes no money is obvious when farm crops dry up in a drought. Good clean drinking water means good health and great abundance of life-giving ch'i.

### 160. Broken burner on the stove.

The cook stove is another symbol of prosperity that needs to be kept clean and in the best operating condition. If a burner is plugged or broken, money problems ensue. Broken burner on the stove also equals loss of money as the ability to cook our food represents abundance as expressed by "cooking on all four burners." It is advisable to utilize all burners for cooking and not just favor one or two as this comes to represent not taking advantage of all your opportunities and just limiting yourself to a few. We are truly blessed if we have a kitchen with a four burner stove and we do not have to cook on Sterno, a camp stove or a one burner hot plate. A six-burner stove is a sign of even greater good fortune.

### 161. Squeaking hinges, floorboards or stairs.

Squeaking hinges or floorboards act upon the subconscious as a constant complaint. WD-40 the hinges or nail down the floor boards and your joints and other systems will flow smoothly and productively. There will be a lot less complaining about petty matters as well. Squeaky hinges always means the people of the house are arguing. Loose or squeaky floorboards usually reflect feelings of uncertainty and insecurity.

### 162. Broken or cracked windows.

Broken or cracked windows can effect the eyes as the windows are symbolically the "eyes of the house." To avoid eye problems replace broken winds immediately. To see "clearly" with inspiration and with vision equals clean, unbroken windows. If you feel you are lacking in "vision," wash and clean your windows.

### 163. Stuck windows.

Stuck windows can effect career and or relationships by encouraging conflict and discord. Struggling to open a window or just not having that option becomes a frustration with a rippling effect though many areas of your life.

### 164. Broken or cracked steps or concrete pathways.

Broken concrete in outside sidewalks, pathways or driveways can have a detrimental influence on bone structures especially the back as would broken stairs and landings. Whether its stiff joints or a broken bone, keep all concrete, if not perfect visually, at least not dangerous or bothersome to walk along. If you have difficulty getting home traversing dangerous and unstable broken wooden stairs or concrete walkways, it willalso be difficult to get other good opportunity to come your way.

### 165. Install water filters.

Install water filters which remove chlorine, heavy metal contaminants, dirt particles, chemicals that have seeped into the ground water as agricultural pesticide/herbicide run off, and in some areas parasites. Ideally you want to filter all the house water. But at least install an under-the-sink filter or a counter top filter for drinking and cooking water and a chlorine removing filter on your shower head as the chlorine/chloroform mist in a shower is easily inhaled and very toxic. There are also chlorine removing filters that hang from the bathtub faucet for running a chlorine-free bath.

It would be nice if civic municipalities would find saner solutions to protecting its citizenry from polluted water instead of exchanging one pollutant for another. Chlorine and the industrial waste fluoride used in toothpaste are just not beneficial for the human body. Notice the notification on toothpaste tubes that warn: "Do Not Swallow."

# Change Your Location, Change Your Life

## Global Feng Shui – Your Astro*Carto*Graphy® Map

Reprinted from the *Maui Special Edition* #2 - Fall 1997 - Stress Free Living Issue

**166. Choosing the best geographical location for you and your family to live.**

In the first issue of Maui Special Edition I introduced you to some basic concepts of feng shui (füng sch'way), the art of placement and design. In this issue I would like to share with you an astrological technique that is similar to feng shui and which I have been introducing to the feng shui community as Global Feng Shui. This technique is called Astro*Carto*Graphy. Where feng shui concerns itself with creating harmony in the immediate home environment by removing obstacles, moving furniture and use of color and symbols, Astro*Carto*Graphy concerns itself to which locations on planet Earth are most harmonious for you to live.

Many of you are familiar with some of the usual ways astrology can be used in self-discovery, understanding relationships and understanding the changes that happen throughout life (transits and progressions). An Astro*Carto*Graphy Map is a map of the world showing exactly where each planet was passing over at the moment of birth. Through my study of Astro*Carto*Graphy, I have found that different locations have different influence making it easier or more difficult to manifest goals and even to resolve personality and health issues.

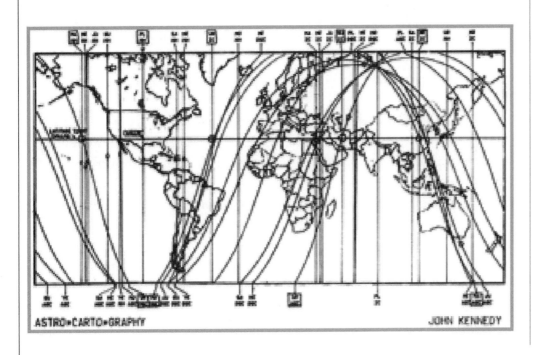

ASTRO*CARTO*GRAPHY                    JOHN KENNEDY

Whenever someone is considering moving to a new location, the Astro*Carto*Graphy Map helps to determine the best location to move to. More frequently, I use this chart when an individual seems unhappy where they are and there is no other astrological reasons to explain why life has been so tough for so long. In these situations it usually turns out the individual is living on an unfavorable planetary line.

The planetary lines that are most favorable are Sun, Jupiter, Venus, Mercury. Sometimes the Moon and Uranus are favoeable especially when combined with the Sun, Jupiter, Venus or Mercury. But never when next to each other or any of the more difficult planets. The lines that are most difficult are Saturn, Pluto, Mars, and usually Neptune. Though favorable lines seem most desirable, some people can use difficult lines to their advantage and sometimes difficult lines aren't as difficult when combined with a more favorable line. But most of the time, difficult lines reflect struggle in career, relationship and even health.

For example: a Saturn-line may be beneficial for a few years in helping someone bring structure into their life. But once they have their 'act together,' the best advice is, "leave." Living on a Saturn-line tends to be depressive, burdensome, alienating, lonely, frustrating, and contractive. Relationships tend to be characterized by rejection and abandonment issues while health problems usually affect the bones, joints and/or teeth.

Pluto-lines can be even worse. Pluto-lines may begin with a wonderful high, even ecstatic highs, but in short time the crest of the wave gives out and there is a heavy fall. Again the advice is, "leave." Pluto-lines tend to affect health by undermining the immune system and by expressing deep core emotional issues as cancers and tumors and other illness that "explode" from deep within the subconscious. On a Pluto-line life is a continuous process of intense inner transformation and karmic cleansing.

Briefly, Mars-lines are contentious, competitive and masculinizing in a negative sense. Head-strong Mars can give headaches and injuries. Uranus can be exciting, innovative and colorful but often ends up as too erratic, nerve wracking and unpredictable. Great for entrepreneurialism and technology but lacking in intimacy and commitment in relationships. Neptune, though creative, imaginative, idealistic and spiritual, tends to be nebulous, anxiety ridden, wishy-washy and rarely sees manifestation with health issues being difficult and hard to diagnose. Both Uranus and Neptune may be more creative, spiritual or romantic when combined with a more favorable planet. The favorable planets bring creativity, popularity, positive relationships, feelings of well-being, and abundance.

So why would anyone choose anything less than the best planetary lines to live on? The karmic necessity to work through specific lessons in life. Where we live fits our patterns. For an individual who has been struggling for years living on a difficult planetary line, looking at an Astro*Carto*Graphy Map usually means they are ready to make a conscious choice to live a more harmonious and fulfilling life.

Of course it should be understood that changing the feng shui of your home or moving somewhere else on planet earth doesn't change your core issues. You always take yourself with you wherever you go. However it should also be understood that by making changes on the physical, you set your intention to change on the spiritual. By moving furniture in your home or changing cities you could remove additional frustrations in resolving these core issues sooner, rather than later. For example: an alcoholic in recovery may find more of an inclination to back-slide in certain locations and more support to grow and change in another.

It would be folly to think that just because you move to or are living on your Venus-line that relationships will be easy or that you will finally meet your soul-mate. Indeed, if you still haven't resolved your core issues of a need to be in control, or your victim-victimizer issues, or whatever issues you have that have made relationships difficult in the past, you will still have them even on your Venus-line. You may even have a relationship that ends in divorce. However, compared to a Mars-line, even the divorce will proceed harmoniously and you will at least part as friends. Whereas on a Mars-line, the relationship is more likely to end in bitterness and with a difficult and bitter court room battle.

For people who travel from location to location there is another technique called Cyclo*Carto*Graphy. This is similar to a transit reading of the birth chart as it shows the changing energy. Former President Carter had Mars in Iran but it wasn't until Pluto went over Iran that this potential aggression exploded in the hostage controversy. Likewise, Pluto was transiting over Dallas at the time Kennedy was assassinated. For the rest of us mere mortals the implications are the same. If you travel to a place during a poor transit, you are likely to experience some form of difficulty reflective of your core issues and evolutionary needs. I made the mistake once of traveling to an otherwise joyous Venus location when Saturn was transiting over head and found myself in a serious accident which put me down for three days. And I was "lucky" (Venus) it was not more serious than that.

Not all astrologers are experienced in Astro*Carto*Graphy Map interpretation nor are the Maps generated on home computers as precise as the

professionally plotted Maps by Astro Numeric Service. These finely produced Maps are 7 1/2" x 15 1/2" and are printed in color on quality paper. I have analyzed hundreds of Maps and can answer all your questions concerning where you presently live; or, if you are planning a move, I can help you choose a place that is best for you and your family. *(See next to last page for ordering information.)*

Acknowledgment: The Astro*Carto*Graphy Map and Manual was developed by astrologer Jim Lewis to whose innovative and inventive Spirit we are greatly indebted.

# Exploring Other Ways to Feng Shui Your Home

*Feng Shui practitioners are artists and technicians of the chi flow,
using any means at their disposal to weave human and environmental chi into
patterns of nourishing energy, which feed and protect every part of your life.*
~~ David Daniel Kennedy, *Feng Shui Tips for a Better Life*

There are many other feng shui techniques in addition to the ones given in this book. All of which have great merit when applied properly. Unfortunately, some people have studied one tradition and, not having studied other systems, presume that their way is the best, the most powerful, and the only way to practice feng shui. It should be understood that whichever system you have invested years of study will prove to be the most dynamic for you. However, being dynamic for you does not preclude that there might be other ways to accomplish the same positive goals.

I have had the good fortune to have studied with many teachers and have gleaned the best they have to offer. I have also had the opportunity to compare their variations. Some students see the contradictions in how different teachers interpret and apply the formulas as perplexing. They want a definitive system. A system without ambiguity. Feng shui is not such a system.

Feng shui is a way of "seeing" the world and a way of analyzing the energetics of a space. It developed over the millennium in different locales and in the context of different cultural influences. Some of it is based on an individual's psychological response to the symbolism of the collective unconscious and some feng shui evaluations are based on mathematical formulas. Some of it is intuitive and some of it is plain common sense.

Understandably, once you bring human sensibilities into any equation there is going to be contradictions and variations. Rather than seeing differing interpretations and approaches as negating the validity of feng shui, I see the variations as liberating. As an indication that there are many ways to solve a problem and many ways to achieve an alignment that will bring opportunity for career success, good health, relationship harmony, and so forth.

It is also a way of understanding that if a problem cannot be solved in one system perhaps a solution can be found in another. As it is unlikely to have 100% perfect feng shui with any system, each system we use adds to the total. Remember, the home is analogous to a container – a container with many holes leaking energy. Our mission is to identify those energy leaks and

then find ways to remedy the situation. However, regardless of which system is utilized, it is important to have a strong foundation. And that is what the feng shui solutions in this book will help you establish.

After choosing your house based on the recommendations in this book, I encourage you to explore other systems, each of which will reveal subtler levels of ch'i flow evaluation. No doubt you will discover other problems to consider and be presented with other opportunities to apply feng shui principles and concepts. With each application the feng shui of your home will grow stronger.

## Flying Star Feng Shui

The two more popular approaches are from the traditional Compass School: Flying Star Feng Shui and Eight Mansion Feng Shui. The Flying Star system is one of the oldest aproaches formulated in northern China. A Flying Star Chart is calculated based on the compass direction plus the construction date of the home corresponding to the 20-year cycle of Jupiter and Saturn. The derived chart becomes the birth chart, or "energy blueprint" of the home.

Experienced Flying Star practitioners can "read" the history of the home and its inhabitants from these charts. They can clearly determine health, relationship and financial circumstances of anyone living in the home. Then based on Annual and even Monthly cycles can predict when good fortune or bad will likely occur. The first compasses were originally developed by Chinese feng shui practicitors to determine the best direction for siting burial plots (Yin Feng Shui). The compass was later used by mariners to navigate the seas and by travelers trying to find their way across unfamiliar lands.

## Eight Mansion Feng Shui

The Eight Mansion system is one of the more recent developments in feng shui having emerged in the latter half of the 19th century. It also utilizes the directions of the compass to determine if the inhabitants are in harmony with a dwelling. Whereas Flying Star Feng Shui used the compass to determine the "alchemy of elements" and by evaluating elemental processes, Eight Mansion Feng Shui uses the compass to determine an individuals best and least favorable directions. An individual's best and least favorable directions are derived from certain formulas based on birth year and gender. These directions are then used to determine whether you will have good fortune based on which way your head is pointing when you sleep, which way you face when you sit at a desk, or as you walk out your front door.

Sometimes it may be suggested that an individuals use a door other than the front door to insure success. Even which way the stove knobs are pointing or which direction you have the rice cooker plugged into the wall can be used to

evaluate if your food will be most nourishing. The location of a bathroom is also considered: will it flush away bad energies or will it flush away good fortune?

## Black Sect Tantric Buddhist Feng Shui

There is also a fusion of classic Chinese ch'i flow analysis with the altar building feng shui and transcendental techniques of the shamanic Bön tradition of Tibet. This system is called Black Sect Tantric Buddhist Feng Shui. This fusion of styles is the innovation of Grandmaster Prof. Thomas Lin Yun. It is this system that is primarily responsible for the emergence of feng shui into the popular awareness of the modern world since the mid-1980's. (The Bön are the indigenous people of Tibet whose spiritual and cultural traditions predate the influx of Buddhist teachings by several thousand years.)

It is the Black Sect use of the Ba-gua that is referred to on page 125 in evaluating the Wealth and Partnership Areas of the home. The Black Sect tradition also places a strong emphasis on prayer, visualization, and intention setting. Prof. Lin Yun refers to the use of the orientation of the Ba-gua to the front door of the house as the "compass of the heart" approach.

Note: This system was originally referred to as the Black Hat Sect. The term "Hat" has since been dropped to avoid confusion with the Black Hat Sect of the Tibetan Tantric Buddhist Kagyu lineage whose titular head is His Holiness the Seventeenth Karmapa. I should also point out that you do not have to be a Buddhist to use the Black Sect approach to feng shui.

## Form School

Among the oldest traditional systems of feng shui is the Form School which originated in the mountainous regions of southern China. It is this analysis of how ch'i flows through the environment that is the foundation for all other feng shui approaches. Form School analysis is the primary basis for the majority of the questions I've included on the Feng Shui Checklist. The basic level of Form School Feng Shui is to analyze how ch'i flows to, through and around an environment. More advanced levels will use the compass to determine what the impact of various geographical features (mountains and rivers) might have on a place of residence.

All teachers regardless of which approach they have mastered agree that without good forms all other systems are less effective. Good forms are needed to activate the elemental interaction of Flying Stars and are needed to support the good intentions of Black Sect remedies. With that in mind I encourage you to continue to explore the many dynamic levels of feng shui wisdom. May your life be blessed with great good fortune.

## My Recommendations:

You will notice sprinkled throughout the text of this book are many quotable quotes from many of the books listed in this Bibliography that help illustrate the principles and concepts of feng shui. I have included these quotable quotes because the author quoted had a perceptive way of verbalizing that I hope will assist in clarification, simplification or in some other way, in a nut shell, to assist you in understanding how feng shui actually works. I highly recommend each and everyone of these wonderful feng shui books.

An asterisk (*) indicates books that were especially important as sources for problems and/or solutions. To these authors thanks, and thanks again.

# Bibliography & Recommended Reading

Carus, Paul. *Chinese Astrology: Early Chinese Occultism.* LaSalle, IL: Open Court Paperback, 1974. (First published in 1907 as *Chinese Thought.*)

Coghill, Roger. *Electro Pollution: How to Protect Yourself Against It.* Wellingborough, England: Aquarian Press, 1990.

* Collins, Terah Kathryn. *The Western Guide to Feng Shui: Creating Balance, Harmony, and Prosperity in Your Environment.* Carlsbad, CA: Hay House, 1996.

* DeAmicis, Ralph & Lahni. *Feng Shui and the Tango in Twelve Easy Lessons.* Cuore Libre Publ., Bryn Athyn, PA: 2001.

Eberhard, Wolfram. *A Dictionary Of Chinese Symbols: Hidden Symbols in Chinese Life and Thought.* London: Routledge & Kegan Paul Ltd, 1986.

Eitel, Ernest J., *Feng-Shui: The Science of Sacred Landscape in Old China.* London: Synergetic Press, 1984. (First published in 1873 by Trübner & Co.)

* Fairchild, Denny. *Healing Homes: Feng Shui Here & Now.* Birmington, MI: WaveField Books, 1996.

Jofre, Michael J., and Robert T. McKusick. *Alive and Well: Neutralizing Environmental Radiations.* Globe, AZ: Biomagnetic Research, Inc., 1991.

* Kennedy, David Daniel. *Feng Shui Tips for a Better Life.* Pownal, VT: Storey Communication, 1998.

Kennedy, David Daniel. *Feng Shui for Dummies.* NY: Hungry Minds, Inc., 2001

Kingston, Karen. *Creating Sacred Space with Feng Shui.* NY: Broadway Books, 1997.

Kwok, Man-Ho with Joanne O'Brien. *The Elements of Feng Shui.* NY: Barnes & Noble, 1991.

Lewis, Jim. *The Astro\*Carto\*Graphy Map Manual.* San Francisco: A\*C\*G, 1976.

* Lim, Prof. Dr. Jes T. *Feng Shui & Your Health: A Guide to High Vitality.* Singapore: Heian Internat'l, 1999.

* Lin, Jami - compiled & edited by. *The Feng Shui Anthology Contemporary Earth Design.* Miami: Earth Design Inc., 1997.

McKusick Charmion R. *In the Claws of the Dragon.* Globe, AZ: Biomagnetic Research, 1997.

Moore, Steve. *The Trigrams of Han: Inner Structures of the I Ching.* Wellingborough, England: Aquarian Press, 1989.

Ni, Hua Ching. *The Book of Changes & the Unchanging Truth.* Malibu, CA: The Shrine of the Eternal Breath of Tao, 1983.

* Post, Stephen. *The Modern Book of Feng Shui: Vitality and Harmony for the Home and Office.* NY: Dell Publ., 1998.

* Rossbach, Sarah. *Interior Design with Feng Shui.* London: Penguin Arkana, 1987.

* SantoPietro, Nancy. *Feng Shui: Harmony by Design.* NY: Berkley Publishing Group, 1996.

SantoPietro, Nancy. *Feng Shui & Health: The Anatomy of a Home.* NY: Three Rivers Press, 2002.

* Skinner, Stephen. *The Living Earth Manual of Feng-Shui: Chinese Geomancy.* London: Penguin Arkana, 1982.

Swartwout, Dr. Glen. *Electromagnetic Pollution Solutions.* Hawaii: Aerai Publ., 1991.

Tanzer, Elliot Jay. *Exercises For the Spiritual Body.* Los Angeles: Self-Published, 1989.

* Thompson, Angel. *Feng Shui: How to Achieve the Most Harmonious Arrangement of Your Home and Office.* NY: St. Martin's Griffen, 1996.

Too, Lillian. *Feng Shui Fundamentals: Wealth.* Boston: Element Books Ltd., 1997.

Too, Lillian. *Lillian Too's Personalized Feng Shui Tips.* Kuala Lumpur: Konsep Books, 1998.

Too, Lillian. *Practical Feng Shui: Symbols of Good Fortune.* Boston: Element Books Ltd., 2000.

Twicken, David, Ph.D, L.Ac. *"Flying Star" Feng Shui Made Easy. Revised Edition.* Lincoln, NE: Writers Club Press, 2000.

Twicken, David, Ph.D, L.Ac. *Treasures of Tao: Feng Shui - Chinese Astrology - Spiritual Qi Gong.* Lincoln, NE: Writers Club Press, 2002.

* Wong, Angi Ma. *Feng Shui Dos and Taboos: A Guide to What to Place and Where.* Palos Verdes, CA: Pacific Heritage Books, 2000.

Wong, Eva. *Feng Shui: The Ancient Wisdom Of Harmonious Living In Modern Times.* Boston: Shambhala Publ., 1996.

* Webster, Richard. *101 Feng Shui Tips for the Home.* St. Paul, MN: Llewelyan Publ., 1998.

* Wu, Dr. Baolin and Jessica Eckstein. *Lighting the Eye of the Dragon: Inner Secrets of Taoist Feng Shui.* NY: St. Martin's Press, 2000.

Wu, Wei. *A Tale of the I Ching: How the Book of Changes Began.* LA: Power Press, 1995.

* Wydra, Nancilee. *Feng Shui: The Book Of Cures.* Chicago: Contemporary Books, 1996.

Ziegler, Holly, MA. Ed. *Sell Your Home FASTER with Feng Shui: Ancient Wisdom to Expedite the Sale of Real Estate.* Arroyo Grand, CA: Dragon Chi Publ., 2001.

# ELLIOT JAY TANZER

### Astrologer, Feng Shui Practitioner,
### Writer and Teacher of Meditation and Metaphysics

**S**ince 1973, Elliot Jay Tanzer has provided astrological services specializing in natal chart interpretations, future forecasts, relationship studies and Astro*Carto*Graphy Map analysis. From 1983 through 1989, after nine years living on the island of Maui, Elliot returned to Los Angeles and established an international reputation while lecturing extensively at major expos, astrological conferences and metaphysical centers. He has also appeared on many radio and television shows. During these years, Elliot taught at Heartwood: California College of the Healing Arts and was awarded an Honorary M.A. in recognition of his many years of synthesis of Eastern and Western mystical traditions.

**F**rom 1990 to January 2000, Elliot again returned to Maui. During these years, Elliot immersed himself in the study of the ancient Chinese art and science of feng shui, published an alternative health and conscious living magazine, and continued to teach classes, and provide astrology readings primarily via the mail and tape-recorded telephone consultations. Elliot again resides in southern California. Since returning to California, Elliot continues to do presentations at expos, conferences and metaphysical centers. He is the co-founder the Integrative School of Feng Shui and is the designer of study guides and other tools for feng shui practitioners. He writes a column for the Los Angeles Whole Life Times, and is finishing his second feng shui book: *The Feng Shui Checklist™ Guidelines for Interior Design*.

**A complete list of lecture and workshop topics, an article archives, and more information about various products and services can be found at Elliot's website: ElliotTanzer.com.**

**TAPE RECORDED ASTROLOGY READINGS BY MAIL**

A Daily Planning Guide for <u>All</u> Sun Signs

The Integrative School of Feng Shui

**Study Guides For the Student / Tools For the Practitioner**
- Feng Shui Master Formulas
- Pre-Calculated Flying Star Charts - Periods 2 ~ 9
- The Interpretations    • Flying Star Tutorial
- Perforated See-Thru Template for Plotting the 8-Compass Directions & the 24-Mountains

**High Quality Lead-Glass Crystals**
_____

**Crystal Catalyst® Beads**

Gifts Certificates Available for Feng Shui or Astrology Consultations

### ORDERING & CONTACT INFORMATION

You can order tools for feng shui practitioners, home study courses, Crystal Catalyst® electronic smog busters, high quality lead-glass crystals, and more copies of this book on-line at:

ElliotTanzer.com

_____

For more information, to find out about up-coming classes, teleconferencing courses, to discuss the mentorship program, or to arrange for a consultation, contact Elliot at:

(310) 281-6798

May you enjoy
a warm or cooling breeze
according to your changing needs.

•

May you enjoy fresh flowing water
to nurture and refresh you
so you may
enjoy good health.

•

May you have abundance
enough to share with others.

•

May you enjoy
sweetness and harmony
in all your relationships.

•

May you enjoy a successful,
satisfying,
creative
and
peaceful
life.

•

May all sentient beings find peace and happiness

and the causes of happiness.

# MAY PEACE PREVAIL ON EARTH

# NOTES

# NOTES

# NOTES

# NOTES